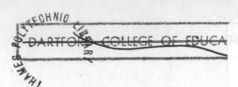

Binder Twine &
Rabbit Stew

To
JOHN WIGGINS and **GEOFF RICH**
who listened to my idea of Paradise.

Binder Twine &
Rabbit Stew

JOAN KENT

BAILEY BROTHERS & SWINFEN LTD
FOLKESTONE

Published in Great Britain by
Bailey Brothers and Swinfen Ltd
1976

SBN 561 00294 0

Printed in Great Britain by offset lithography by
Billing & Sons Ltd, Guildford, London and Worcester

Contents

INTRODUCTION

Confident that she had long since finished having babies, my middle aged mother gave the old iron rocking cot to gipsies picking fruit in the orchard. By the end of that summer she suspected she had been over-optimistic. The gipsies gave it back.

When I arrived one Primrose Day in the early nineteen-twenties Mum considered naming me after the flower, but Dad was determined that their 'afterthought' would not go through life labelled 'Primmy'. Even at the tiny bud stage I bore no resemblance to a rose.

'Home' was an old farmhouse set amid the patchwork of meadows, fields and orchards that lie between the wooded North Down hills and the marshes of East Kent.

A large family and a farmhouse made Mum's work never-ending, so Dad and my three elder brothers often took me with them as they worked around the farm. A harvest wagon made a mobile playpen. Happiness was to sleep sun-warmed, wrapped in my father's coat.

Dad used his horses to haul timber from the nearby woodlands. As soon as I could manage the linen covered 'indestructable' buttons that prevented the 'tail-board' of my calico drawers from dropping, I was allowed to ride on the lumbering timber tugs with my brothers and spent day after day playing happily in the summer woods.

Winter-wrapped and snug beside a tree-feller's fire, I sat with the secretive silence of pine plantations whispering all around me, drinking down folk story superstitions and smoky, condensed-milk sweetened tea.

Blessed with parents rich in everything but money, I had a free, unfettered childhood. Mum, like a warm, soft fronted, bulgy bolster, cushioned the sharper corners of my small world with comfort, common sense and love.

The blind mare's colt was a favourite companion. Some of my best friends were sheep.

School was like chilblains, something to be endured; 'The Scholarship' a sword of doom hovering above my head.

INTRODUCTION

The written part was easy. The 'oral' assessment of my intelligence hinged on my ability to arrange toy furniture in a 'two up, two down' dolls' house. With all four rooms furnished, I had a miniature toilet suite to spare. A helpful adjudicator suggested one upper compartment could be a bathroom. Living where piped water was the dream of a slumberous rural council, and main drainage or indoor sanitation unheard of, I rejected that theory out of hand.

"Who would want to cart hot water jugs and lavatory buckets up and down stairs?" I queried. I did not pass. 'If, however, Dad cared to pay half fees, I was worthy of etc., etc.' Even at reduced rates, my school fees would buy enough pig meal to fatten a score of piglets into porkers. One could get mighty hungry trying to put text books between two hunks of bread.

The depression of the 'thirties' was a hungry rat nibbling Dad's capital away. He found safe city jobs for my brothers, my sisters who were still unmarried went away to work. The kitchen table that had always seemed short on elbow room developed areas of empty space.

I grew tall and spindly as a bean plant in a cellar. The ground had an increasing tendency to come up and hit me in the face. Pronounced 'a sick girl' by the village doctor, he prescribed fresh air, sunshine and rest. At thirteen I had spent my last days at school.

Since I spent hours reading in a sheltered corner of the orchard, it took no effort to keep an eye on the grazing sheep. By fourteen I had become chiropodist and midwife to a flock of Southdown ewes. I could not even contemplate leaving my hard-pressed parents. This was our land. My roots belonged there too.

Butcher's meat was a 'sometimes on Sunday' luxury. We ate rabbit instead. No small farmer would waste money getting farm equipment repaired if wire, or the twine that was used to bind sheaves of corn, would mend it. These then were the years when poverty and hard work were leavened with neighbourliness and laughter, the days of binder twine and rabbit stew.

I had been in love with the blacksmith's eldest son from my schooldays. We married on one of his wartime leaves from the R.A.F.

It is not everyone's idea of honeymoon bliss to go harvesting in company with land girls, ancient countrymen and a platoon of soldiers, but the weather was dry and the Germans were unloading incendiary bombs at night.

A few more leaves, then an overseas posting took Alan east of Suez for three and a half years. I continued helping Dad, awaiting his return.

One day I noticed a group of men out in Barn Field, and asked what they were doing.

"Just looking at likely post war housing sites," was their answer. For my parents it was the beginning of the end.

Demobbed, Alan embarked on a career 'in the public service'. This entailed much moving around the country. I have planted gardens from Devon to the Durham border, expressing a need to 'scratch about on the land'.

With steel-grey rain falling on the slate-grey roofs of a less salubrious area of Cardiff, I read an article in the local evening paper extolling the paradise of living in a prepackaged, plastic-tiled type world.

Watching a smoke pall drift over from the steel works, I realised that while I had been raising my own family, my country way of life had been swept away. Farming methods, unaltered for centuries, had been transformed into a mechanised industry. I scribbled down fragmentary memories of the little paradise I once knew.

Two days later, it was published in the South Wales Echo.

John Wiggins, then the editor, wrote suggesting that I sent more articles, and went to see his colleague, 'Geoff' Rich. Encouraged by the friendly, down to earth approachability of all the Editorial and Features staff at Thomson House, I started writing, and so a long and happy association with the

INTRODUCTION

South Wales Echo began.

We moved so often that the furniture creaked whenever a removal van went past, then, almost miraculously, we got a posting back to Kent, where we began.

We bought a little house with a wilderness of a garden, and wandered round the old haunts we had known. It was almost thirty years since I had last met one of my father's neighbours, but recognition was instantaneous.

"What are you doing dressed up like a Sunday tea-cake, and us just starting mowing hay?" he enquired. It was as if I had never been away.

JOAN KENT.
Beam Ends.
1976

Hayforks
and blisters

Recruiting extra labour for hay-making presented few problems for my father: he had a home grown work force of his own. Being a member of our family was like conscription into an army where no one was excused duties, and anyone feigning sickness ran the risk of being dosed with one of Mum's action-packed remedial brews. Instantly effective, these were far more tiring and painful than hard work.

My sisters were expected to muster to the hayfield soon after they got home from work, and like unsuspecting fish that swim too close to the engulfing tentacles of an octopus, any young man trying to make the running with one of 'Harry's girls' found himself red faced and perspiring, pitching hay.

The weaker, less interested lovers soon lost heart, while those who stayed the course were reckoned to have proved that they had honourable intentions. Three weeks of physically exhausting hay-making ensured that this was so.

My brothers were pretty luckless too. Disillusioned, one

1

girl friend wrote to say that since she might just as well have got engaged to a pitchfork, she was returning the thirty shillings that my brother had given her to buy a ring. In future, the boy behind the bacon slicer in the Colonial Stores would provide the excitement and sparkle that her life had hitherto lacked. My brother, praying for rain and the chance of reconciliation, sang soulful songs of unrequited love that unsettled the horse in the wagon shafts and made the loaders curse.

The tentacles of family sometimes spread wider, and uncles, aunts and cousins from the town, thinking that they were being invited to spend idyllic summer days in rustic revelry, soon gathered blisters and sunburn as well as hay. Aunts who preferred cookery to boiling themselves in the sun found that there were mountains of food to contend with in Mum's kitchen and worked far harder than they ever did at home.

There was a definite art in building a haystack. First came a base of faggots of wood, topped by a layer of straw. As the stack was built up, the sides had to be straight, the corners square, and the centre packed in tight, layer after layer. This was called 'treading the stack', and providing that we could haul, shove, and push all sixteen stone of my Aunty Bet up the ladder, we had the best stack-treader in the business. Given half-an-hour just wandering around the top of the stack, Aunty Bet could compress the height of it by at least three rungs of the ladder.

By the time I was old enough to be on eye-ball level to a horse's nostrils, I was detailed to lead the horse in the wagon shafts from haycock to haycock and call out, "Stand hard above," to the chap on the load.

When my legs were long enough to reach the foot lever on the horse-rake I was promoted and, perched on the rake behind a placid old mare, wandered across and across the new mown hay, raking it up into lines.

Phyl, the old mare, was replaced by a beautiful strawberry roan horse and, apart from a tendency to go around in circles, he seemed a docile beast. Plodding around a ten acre field

2

with Gipsy in the shafts of the rake, I began to sing.

It had a traumatic effect on the horse. After circling on its hind legs, it did a spot of dressage, went into a waltz routine, took a bow, and attempted to lie prone. That is not easy with a hay-rake hitched on behind.

We concluded that Gipsy had been a circus horse, but it was ego-deflating to be continuously warned,

"For heaven's sake girl, don't sing."

Boy friends became husbands, girl friends became wives, and our kitchen table seemed to grow larger as our family shrank. In time there were only three places to set for meals. Dad's, Mum's and my own. Cushioning them against the farming depression, Dad found safe jobs for his sons and hay-making became a case of catch as catch can.

But if it was a time of poverty, it was the time of neighbourliness too.

War brought conscription and the younger men went away. We had to rely on casual labour for carrying crops and this was mostly old men who seemed to hibernate between threshing time and spring. There were some odd old characters among them too.

There was Captain Puddington, an eccentric ex-mariner, who hoisted and lowered the flag from a pole stuck up in his apple tree at dawn and sunset each day and kept his wife confined to ship, only allowing her shore leave to collect his rum ration from the Hare and Hounds.

Another stalwart was tobacco-chewing Jimmy Spit, who brought expectorating to so fine an art that he could be on target at twenty paces. His comrade, old Tommy Yellows, was willing enough to work, it was his bladder that was weak.

If possible we used to arrange it so that Captain Puddington loaded while the other men pitched. It was courting disaster to have them up aloft and if the necessity arose, one walked well clear or wore a wide brimmed hat.

By the next hay-making season, some of the farm buildings were providing temporary billets for troops evacuated

4

from Dunkirk. Grey-faced, with eyes that had looked at hell, they had come back from a world that had gone berserk, while we continued gathering the hay harvest in the same old timeless way.

With food production vital, under-manned farmers could ask the army for seasonal help. Dad applied, stating his requirements as four or five men.

An enormous Matador transport, loaded with a platoon of soldiers in full battle order, trundled across the field.

They set up tents, field kitchen, and latrines under the trees and on the following morning, a sergeant, who could have used his larynx to crush gravel, bellowed his orders, "Get fell in there. Shoulder pitchforks. By numbers. Operation Hayseed, begin!"

Once it was clearly understood that I was there to gather hay and not roll in it, the soldiers became a bunch of homesick chaps with photos of wives and families to be admired, and by inviting their partners down for a visit Mum must have saved more than one or two marriages that were on the blink.

Captain Puddington was no longer helping us. He had constructed a crow's nest in his apple tree and spent his time on look-out with a spy glass and a marline spike, convinced that we were about to be subjugated by the German Fleet. He often reported the sighting of enemy cruisers, although the nearest deep water was a good day's march away.

It wasn't seaborne attack that bothered us, but the trigger-happy Luftwaffe pilot attempting to paralyse Britain's war effort by straffing a tractor-driving girl and two old men on a load of hay. This had a disastrous effect on Tommy Yellows, who worked in some discomfort for the rest of the day.

Relating his experiences to the soldiers who were surfacing from taking cover in the hedge, Jim Spit declared, "By gob, if it had been bullets I was chewing instead of baccy, I'd 'ave shot the booger down."

The soldiers were gone. The Land Army girls were a hard working, happy-go-lucky crowd, but neither they nor we were prepared for the additional labour force that helped us next. These were Italian prisoners of war and within an hour of arrival three Land Army girls had gone screaming indoors to show Mum where they had been pinched.

A pitchfork poised at the right angle has more uses than turning hay, and the language difficulty was soon overcome.

Efficient, methodical German prisoners, shell-shocked soldiers, each group in turn helped stack our hay in those grey years.

It seemed at first that we would go back to the traditional way of hay-making when peace returned but, walking around the implement section of the first post-war county show, we saw balers, rakes and lifts: monster machines that could mechanise the operation.

"Fine for prairie farmers," said my Dad, "but can you imagine any good farmer ruining his hay crop by packing it up in rolled square lumps. It will never catch on here."

The miracle kit

When mid-winter lethargy covers the countryside and the sun goes back to bed soon after it gets up, the daylight rarely sheds the last damp blanket of twilight. This makes life in the isolated cottages and farms dreary in the extreme.

Before the 'electric' came, winter was far worse.

The one link with the busy world beyond the dark, dank lanes, breaking the monotony of the long lamp-lit evenings, was the radio. It was called the wireless then, and regarded as little short of miraculous.

With the standard wage for a farm labourer at 32s. 6d. a week, the wireless was an extravagance not easily attained.

Although our family was in slightly easier circumstances, the outlay of unnecessary expenditure was something to be churned and chewed over by my parents for months.

Then my brother saw an advertisement in a newspaper. 'Build your own wireless set', it read. 'Full instructions for easy assembly. Complete kit and cabinet. Success assured or money returned.'

7

THE MIRACLE KIT

To illustrate that it was child's play to construct the kit there was a picture of a curly-headed moppet clutching a soldering iron and surrounded by a group of adults transfixed in attitudes of astonishment.

Hardly surprising this, for in front of them was a wireless cabinet from which a volcano of crotchets, quavers, and treble clefs erupted across the page.

If a small girl could do it, surely it was not beyond the combined brain power of my three elder brothers to assemble a wireless and make it work.

Days extended into weeks as we waited, not knowing quite what to expect or how it would arrive; then a railway van delivered a crate the size of a tea chest.

Grand-daddy of all do-it-yourself construction kits, each part was lifted from a cocoon of wood shavings and laid out on the kitchen table.

Subdued into unusual silence I sat, a small, incredulous spectator, anxious to catch the first glimpse of the little black notes on stalks escaping from the bakelite chassis that my brother Harold was joining together.

No miracles occurred that night, or on the subsequent evenings either. For days we ate our meals crowded up together at one end of the kitchen table, since the wireless kit could not be cleared or disturbed.

Mum complained about the inconvenience incessantly, but four pounds worth of components, not to mention the seven shillings 'carriage paid home', was far too much to risk the loss of any pieces by moving them about.

Wallowing in strange-sounding phrases like 'tuning condenser', 'wave-change switch' 'high and low tension batteries' and 'rectifiers and transformers' made little sense to any of us.

Mum, trying to be helpful, bent close to study a diagram and a powerful magnet on the loudspeaker system pulled all the hairpins from her head, releasing the coils of her long hair to fall round her shoulders.

She distrusted the wireless after that and gave it a wide

berth until all the pieces were safely inside the cabinet and the lid screwed shut.

At last six enormous valves were pushed into their holders, the batteries were connected, then faintly, but just discernable, we heard a low-pitched hum. Now all that it needed to make it work was an aerial, but this was not a matter to be undertaken lightly.

My brother Stan climbed to the top of the copper beech tree in the yard and, hauling up a long pole, lashed it to the top of the trunk.

There was a theory that the mysterious sound waves could dissipate themselves into the tree and kill off all the leaves, so a porcelain insulating cup was joined into the wire where it cleared the branches.

There was another insulator where the lead-in wire to the set entered the kitchen window, put there because without it sounds and signals from far-off places could infiltrate into the very walls of our home.

The aerial wire swung high above the washing line, announcing to our little world that we had joined the listening elite.

But any machine that could pluck music from the air and conjure up foreign-sounding voices must surely attract lightning and thunder-bolts or something worse, so a simple knife switch that earthed the aerial was fastened to the window frame. Each night the lightning conductor switch was religiously turned down, in much the same way as old-time horsemen hung hag-stones on stable doors to prevent witches hagriding their horses in the church-yard still of the night.

There were those who were convinced that anything that could relay voices of people hundreds of miles away, must upset the cycle of the seasons, and our wireless was blamed for every storm or heavy shower that came.

Any attempt to explain electro-magnetic waves travelling across the ether only made it worse. Wasn't ether the stuff used in hospital operations? People who sat listening to the wireless obviously risked being put to sleep.

Nevertheless, Mum would kneel in front of the wireless cabinet, carefully trying to synchronise the two tuning dials to capture the signals from an elusive station.

"Fancy, Radio Hilversum! That accordian music is coming all the way from a country where everyone walks round in wooden clogs." I marvelled with her.

We would sit with our feet on the big brass fender, sharing the warmth of the huge old kitchen range in the chimney corner with two or three cats, a line of working boots and coats put round to dry and friends who had walked muddy fields to share in listening to the miracle of sound.

As time went on wireless sets became commonplace, but our old home-made set still worked and Mum became more expert at finding the Continental stations for our interest and entertainment.

I remember listening to a stirring military band, followed by a wild cheering and someone hysterically shouting in a harsh-sounding foreign language.

"That's coming from Hamburg. Must be that new Hitler chap that's taken over in Germany", Mum said, but Dad told her to change the station or turn it off.

"Sounds more like an underworked, excitable, penned bull looking at a passing herd of cows. That man sounds like trouble in anybody's language. He'll need watching, mark my words."

Mum shut the wireless off, but the shouts of 'Sieg Heil' that we heard that night in the nineteen-thirties was a sound the world would grow to fear.

The wireless was something to be savoured and not squandered by the womenfolk idling during the day. That would run down the high tension battery, heavy, awkward and big as a fair-sized roasting tin. The low-tension wet battery, or accumulator, needed recharging every ten to fourteen days.

These were cumbersome to carry and tipped over at the slightest provocation, making acid holes or staining anything the liquid touched.

THE MIRACLE KIT

The garage at the far side of Lockley Green, which was nothing more than a hand-cranked petrol pump and a tin shed, did a battery-recharging service.

One enterprising boy, who grew up to own a transport fleet, started up in business collecting accumulators for recharging in a massive old twin pram, wheeling it over to the garage and bringing the charged batteries back.

Progress, creeping at a snail's pace, reached the village, first with piped water and gas, then electricity came striding across the fields on pylon stilts and creosoted poles.

We had a new radio set and discovered that 'London Speaking' people did not suffer from permanent catarrh, nor did real music sound as if it had been trapped in an old treacle tin before it dispersed itself across the ether.

The gamekeeper happened to be in our kitchen soon after we got our new set and he told us an unbelievable tale.

'His Lordship' had just come back from London, where he had witnessed a remarkable demonstration from the B.B.C. He had seen a radio set with a glass screen in front and not only had he listened to the broadcasters, but watched them moving on the screen, and them at least three streets away. Videograph or television, it was called.

Mum and Dad both said that a wireless set that could make moving pictures was something they would believe when they saw one for themselves.

I wish they had.

Unwillingly to school

There have been more changes in the pattern of country life in the last quarter of a century than in any time in our traceable history.

Agricultural methods have advanced so rapidly that many landworkers now operating in the highly mechanised farming industry once cultivated the land with implements that had remained virtually unaltered since the middle ages.

This quiet revolution has affected every aspect of rural community life, and nowhere is this more noticeable than in the changed conditions for country school-children.

I sometimes see a group of animated infants eagerly awaiting the arrival of a mini-bus to transport them to school. At mid-afternoon they disembark, chattering like magpies, clutching poster-painted masterpieces and happily relating the day's happenings at school. For young children attending the pre-war village school it was a different story.

There was no school transport and in mid-winter children from outlying farms and cottages left their homes before day-

12

MARTIN LAW.

J·K·

break to walk the goblin-haunted muddy miles to school, not daring to be late. It would be dusk before they returned.

I was lucky, for although I lived almost two miles from the school by road, there was a short cut across the fields and I had two pairs of winter boots and a waterproof warm coat.

For other schoolmates who had to make do with one pair of boots, the muddy farm tracks meant perpetual cold and wet feet while chilblains were a seasonal plague.

The standard farm-hand's wage at that time was 32s.6d a week. This might be augmented if the wife did field work cutting winter cabbage or picking brussels sprouts.

Any offspring too advanced to stay strapped in a pram at the end of the cabbage rows was 'put on the roll' at school. These toddlers trekked to school with their bigger brothers and sisters.

The school-master was a Mr. Steelman, and never was an individual more aptly named. He was small of stature, with a cadaverous face and iron-grey hair. The cold grey eyes that glared through his steel-rimmed pince-nez spectacles invoked the same hypnotic effect on a timid four- or five-year-old as a stoat outstaring a cowering baby rabbit.

He was assisted by his wife, a dessicated woman with bony hard-hitting hands, who habitually wore a mouldy green hand-woven skirt and two thick black drooping cardigans all through the year.

She needed them in winter, too. The entire school was housed in one long high-pitched draughty room. Near a wooden partition, jammed into permanent disuse, a free-standing circular combustion stove sulked fumes or glowed red-hot, depending on the direction of the wind.

In addition there was an open fire at the 'babies' end of the room. And babies the first year pupils were. Walking long distances to school, often coming from families with incomes that could barely provide the basic nutritional necessities, it was no wonder that they frequently keeled over off their seats asleep.

UNWILLINGLY TO SCHOOL

The old feudal social system still lingered on in our community and this percolated down to the 'babies' class in the school. The higher one's parents rated in the status scale, the nearer to the fireplace one sat.

Pride of place went to a girl named Jessica, the daughter of 'His Lordship's' steward. She came to school wrapped in a travelling rug in a wicker-work basket carrier on the back of an estate hand's bike and I detested everything about her, from the sausage curls in her auburn hair, to the mud-free soles of her brown kid buttoned boots.

Next came the son of a prosperous farmer, the postmaster's daughter, the blacksmith's tubby son, an overweight girl from the local inn, and then myself. Six to a form we sat, and I can only think that I made the front rank on sufferance, because Dad happened to be a stalwart of the parish council.

The other five children were all plump and I invariably cliff-hung to the edge of the form by half a cheek.

Lessons were written on slates and erased with the aid of spit and sleeve, or the hanky that we had to wear pinned to the front of our frocks and jerseys. At all other times we sat with folded arms or with our hands placed on the top of our heads.

Singing lessons were not conducive to a love of music. Each May we practised for Empire Day. The local dignitaries always attended the school celebration and Jessica of the auburn curls always sang the solo part.

One year when she came out in spots, three of us lesser fry were detailed to sing her parts. The hymn was 'All Things Bright And Beautiful' and I was supposed to sing solo in the verse that runs 'The rich man in his castle, The poor man at his gate, God made them high and lowly, And ordered their estate'. This I did not believe, and not even our sycophant headmaster could make the words come from my mouth. I sang loud 'La-La-Las' instead and suffered later on.

Although I curtsied to our honoured visitors with all the rest, Dad was warned that his youngest daughter was showing

15

some very radical tendencies that would need to be severely curbed.

We did get cheap school milk, but school dinners were a future dream as far as our school was concerned. Looking back, the contents of our dinner bags demonstrated the poverty of our times.

Again I was fortunate. My mother used to fill a pint enamel milk can with either soup or rabbit stew, to supplement bread, cheese and fruit. Many had to make shift with dripping sandwiches, or bread and mixed-fruit jam.

Many a school dinner came to grief by falling off the prongs of an improvised toasting fork pushed through the bars of the guard round the 'babies' room fire.

By grace and favour, my can of rabbit stew was heated on the top of the combustion stove and various other 'dinner children' were afforded a quick dip of their stale crusts in my stew. It soaked up the runny part and I was left with the solid bits in which I would often gain remnants of someone else's fish paste spread.

Under the guise of being taught 'housecraft', the older girls were sent across to the schoolmaster's house. There they were taught bed-making, laundry and rudimentary cooking by his wife. Cookery consisted of making onion soup and baked egg custard, a basic in our teacher's diet.

When I reached the dizzy academic heights of being in 'Standard Six', I too was instructed in these culinary arts, and was happy to discover that, unknown to other pupils, the big girls working in the school house kitchen had been waging a secret war of retaliation and revenge.

Solemnly, each one added her contribution to the custard, and I spat with the rest.

The schoolmaster's moods became more and more eccentric and then quite suddenly he was gone. His replacement was a gentle, spell-binding man who showed us that our narrow world was a storehouse of country lore and historically interesting things.

16

He taught us that words were wondrous weapons and talked about our heritage of the unchanging land.

A branch of the county library is open in the old schoolrooms two afternoons each week. Its musty atmosphere still smells of chalk and steaming leather boots, conjuring memories of children of another age who are still young enough to be active in the new.

Cooking them dratted germs

To Mum, illness was like a bad smell on the landing: something to be dealt with ruthlessly, effectively and without wasting precious time.

She took anything short of actual surgery in her stride and her simple remedies brought about some speedy cures, possibly because being 'made well' was such an uncomfortable business.

It was sheer lunacy to cough in the first few weeks of the year. In addition to the usual sugar soaked in Friars Balsam and eucalyptus that took the plating off the spoon and left the victims convinced they were the unwilling stooge in a fire-eating act, there was an 'after Christmas' bonus.

Having regained your breath and wiped your streaming eyes, your mouth was filled with a great dollop of goose grease.

Willingly, or by the sheer necessity of having to breathe despite a firmly gripped nose, you swallowed it and then submitted to having goose grease plastered on your chest.

A distinct smell of sage and onion wafted from under your

liberty bodice well into spring.

It only needed Mum's hand to feel a hot forehead and we were off again! Two dozen onions and a few chillies were boiled up in an iron pot while sand-filled stone jars that had been heated in the oven warmed the patient's bed.

In a flannel nightshirt topped by a woollen cardigan and cocooned in the bed clothes, even the most rebellious knew better than to refuse the basin of pepped-up onions.

Mum called it, 'cooking them dratted germs'. While perspiration oozed from every pore, bed and steaming patient were covered by Dad's best horse rug. Dad disliked the idea but the horses never seemed to object.

Strains, sprains and circulatory troubles were easily dealt with. Horses and humans simply shared the same bottle of embrocation, Mum's contention being that if the cure hurt more than the complaint, it would all feel better soon.

Chilblains called for a slightly different method of approach. The first line of attack was oil of wintergreen and salt, massaged in with all the delicacy of a rotary sanding machine.

Stage two involved first catching a sheep and pulling out a handful of its fleece. Having wrapped one's swollen toes in the odorous greasy wool, how you got your shoes on afterwards was a problem that you worked out for yourself.

Inner cleanliness was a fetish with our Mum and every Saturday evening saw the family downing massive doses of liquorice. Not for us the luxury of a long lie-in on Sunday mornings!

Spots, pimples, and being in love were all symptoms of the same complaint, all requiring a mixture for cooling down the blood. This was obtained by mixing the yellow powder of 'flowers of sulphur' with treacle ladled from a barrel in the corn shed.

The same stuff was administered to horses with a poor or 'staring' coat. I never saw a horse with pimples and it did nothing for our hair, so I don't imagine that it can have worked in reverse.

Sometimes Mum discovered interesting knowledge by accident, and, while she was delighted when it proved to be of practical use, her patients were sometimes grudging in their thanks.

She knew why misery masked the pretty face of a querulous young wife who called each week to purchase eggs and a recent observation led Mum to think she could possibly help the girl.

There was a whispered confidential chat and the customer departed with two bottles under the dozen eggs in her rush basket.

Mum disclosed that when she had strained and bottled the Morella cherry wine, the behaviour of our normally placid farmyard fowls, after they pecked at the fermented cherries, led her to believe that the juice might be particularly potent.

Mum's therapy obviously worked, for everyone was delighted with the news of an impending arrival. But happiness is a fleeting thing.

When the couple had four children in as many years they placed the blame on Mum and developed a kind of hate fixation for our innocent cherry trees.

Mum immediately imposed sanctions on that year's crop of cherry wine and gave it to an honoured few, only those in a state of wedlock qualifying. Definitely excluded was Aunt Bet's husband, who needed no encouragement and had a roving eye for a pretty barmaid.

When the juice from the fleshy leaves of the plant that flourished on our lavatory roof failed to cure a sudden crop of warts that covered my hands and arms, Mum called in a specialist.

She had seen his handiwork before and had great respect for an old man who most people regarded as being little more than a worthless tramp.

We called him 'Cockle Billy,' for he eked out an existence gathering shellfish from the foreshore and transporting them to nearby towns in a squeaking, buckle-wheeled old pram.

COOKING THEM DRATTED GERMS

He bought my warts for a shilling piece and buried them under the flowering currant bush. My warts vanished and for years I trod gingerly near that bush, afraid that I might find a crop of warts growing like mushrooms from the ground.

Mum had an uncanny instinct for sensing when any of her scattered family was sick and we attributed this to the fact that she had a Romany grandmother.

I often wonder if that could also account for the most remarkable bit of home nursing that I have ever seen.

The old threshing machines that travelled from farm to farm before the advent of combine harvesters all had 'Threshing Johnnies' who slept rough, lived rough and were as hard as nails.

Their job was to cut the bonds from the sheaves with vicious sharp hooked knives and feed the corn into the revolving drums on top of the machine.

One of these men once cut his hand where thumb and forefinger meet, slicing it almost to the bone. He lost balance and caught his injured hand in the machine.

The thresher stopped and he was assisted to the bench beside the farmhouse door. In his filthy state tetanus was a real danger and he was losing too much blood, but terror of 'the 'orspital' far outweighed his fear of bleeding to death.

Mum came bustling on the scene and without a word tore the strings off her apron, tied one round his wrist and the other round his upper arm. I was detailed to find an old but freshly laundered sheet while Mum sorted out the mangled flesh with a gentle, infinite care.

She went into the corn store and came out carrying the biggest cobwebs she could find. Before an open-mouthed, goggle-eyed girl and a group of men who were sure that now they had seen everything, she slapped the cobwebs over the wounds. She bound the patient's hand and fixed a sling to rest his arm, then went about her daily tasks as if she did that sort of thing every day.

She would never discuss the incident except for one occasion when she told me that instinctively she had remembered hearing an old lady talking of the same sort of situation and remedy.

Within a week or two that hand was completely healed. Don't ask me how — I only wish I knew.

We smiled at my old Mum and her cures, but they were based on common sense, confidence and the most unpleasant brew she could concoct.

Now we queue in overcrowded waiting rooms, breathing in each other's germs and spreading those we have ourselves, to get a bottle of strawberry flavoured linctus that we take religiously for the first three doses then leave with the row of other medicines on the shelf.

A gallon of Friar's Balsam, a gallon of eucalyptus, half a hundredweight of sugar lumps, someone with the personality of my old Mum to dish it out, and present day surgery queues would vanish like mist before the sun.

Please, no goose grease for me though, because I don't wear a liberty bodice any more.

Whitsun Fete

Whit Monday was always something of a relief. The ordeal of having to keep the new Whit Sunday dress clean and intact, the suspense of wondering if by some mischance I had been included in the list of Sunday school prize-winners, was over.

On the only occasion that I was selected to scramble over children's outstretched legs into the aisle and tread the never-ending strip of grey coconut-matting, the vicar consulted both his list and the flyleaf of my prize to verify my name, declaring that it justified his belief in miracles.

But that was yesterday and now it was Whit Monday, traditionally the day for the vicarage fete and children's treat.

All morning long Vicarage Lane was busy with wagons transporting chairs and crockery from the village hall to the vicarage paddock. Men with mallets sorted out tangled ropes and struggled to erect the large marquee, while harrassed ladies scuttled round, putting old and faded curtains over trestles and setting out their stalls.

Order always emerged out of chaos soon enough for the

23

flags of empire to flutter from the tops of tents and between the avenue of trees in the vicarage drive before the
grand opening.

After dinner I was released from the rag curlers which
corrugated my scalp but did nothing for my hair. Scrubbed,
polished and magnificent in yesterday's new dress, I went to
the fete, complete with mug and spoon.

All along Vicarage Lane the strains of a band, giving forth
with *Blaze Away,* heightened the excitement. My two older
sisters, somewhat hampered by their first pairs of silk stockings, struggled to keep my pace.

'Her Ladyship' always declared the fete open, economically
wearing the same 'cabbage rose' hat and using the same speech
every year.

It meant that everyone automatically clapped or laughed
at the right time, but could concentrate on which stall was
likely to offer the best value for the spending money that
burned in the pocket or was clutched, sticky, in the hand.

The sultry sun shone down upon the sweating City Silver
Band, roasting in their splendid martial uniforms as they
played *Colonel Bogey, The Merry Widow,* and selections from
Show Boat, with all the fervour their panting lungs permitted.

There was little time to visit all the stalls, so I by-passed the
ones that would not sell out quickly and concentrated on
buying a halfpenny glass of shocking-pink raspberry sherbert,
a toffee apple and some sticks of peppermint twist, all sticky
and gooey in the heat.

The postmistress presided over the sweet stall. The ogey-
pogey-eyes, the liquorice chews and giant humbugs, along
with all the other old stock that had hung fire on her shelves
all winter, were dusted off and sold at a cut rate.

The band stopped playing to let the schoolmaster attempt
to blow his whistle through a megaphone. Feeling very im-
portant, those of us who were 'in it' ran across the erstwhile
sacred turf of the vicarage lawn and went into the house.

In a kitchen that smelled of beeswax and stale cabbage we

put on crepe-paper dresses, the wings and the crowns of silver paper stars, so laboriously made at school.

The leading lady howled with nerves, forgetting every line she ever learned, and I was glad. I knew my part quite well because in fact it consisted of one word, and then I got it wrong!

While we were dressing, a heavy shower, thundery but of short duration, sent people running to the shelter of the tents, but the sun came out as we were led out through the vegetable garden and through the wicket gate to the shrubbery that was the backcloth to the tennis court, our open air theatre.

A deputation of anxious Mums sent the vicar as spokesman to tell the schoolmaster that their precious daughters must not perform barefooted as he had intended.

Dancing around on damp grass would do quite hideous things to growing girls' insides and the least we could expect was galloping consumption.

The schoolmaster suggested that it was the perfect solution to his overcrowded classroom, but glanced at the hovering gaggle of mothers, fearsome in their cherry-laden hats, and gave ground.

I looked down at the brown buttoned boots that encased my ankles and was delighted to realise that Titania would be forced to trip on to the stage in knee-high, black lace-up boots.

Oberon and Snug outraged our fairy dignity by suggesting that they could see our navy bloomers underneath. A battle royal ensued and I was hauled out of a heap of rotting, rain-sodden lawn clippings, my paper dress soggy and torn, dripping dye on to what ever it touched.

Only my protruding ears prevented the crown of stars from completely covering my face.

The schoolmaster's long-suffering wife, prompt-book in hand, crouched in a wet laurel bush. The schoolmaster announced that his pupils would perform Act 3 of A Midsummer Night's Dream and the old horn gramophone, wobbling on a rickety cane table, started up the music of Mendelsohn's Overture.

Like early Christian martyrs we were pushed into the arena and I tripped across the lawn in my drooping paper dress and brown button boots.

The maypole dancers followed us, weaving their coloured lattice patterns. Being left-handed, with a tendency to turn in the opposite direction to everyone else, I had once succeeded in getting the ribbons in a hopeless knot and was forbidden to attempt the feat again.

The Brownies' action songs were not for me either. Brown Owl once fell over one of our straying cows asleep on her front porch.

She landed in the evidence of its visit and that started a feud.

The children's acts were planned to let the stallholders and band have an early tea but, soon after the Brownies let 'Little Redwing' rest in peace, the band struck up with the *Grand March* from *Aida*.

Every child in the village, be they Church, Chapel, Catholic or Hottentot, lined up in a procession to the children's tea.

While the younger children munched their way through piles of sandwiches, cakes, and jelly, melting and tasting waxy in a cardboard dish, the older folk slipped off to have their tea.

The echelons of society were clearly defined. The elite were invited to drawing room tea in the vicarage and it cost them two shillings and sixpence. Farmers and tradesfolk sat on the verandah and were charged two shillings. Tea on the lawn cost one shilling and sixpence, while lesser folk stood drinking penny cups of tea from the urn and bought buns from a stall.

After tea, the coconut shies, the hoopla, skittles and other games of chance came into their own. 'Bowling for the pig' was a great attraction and many a cottage sty was cleared on the offchance of winning it.

The pig, a runt from our blue sow's last litter, had been squealing all afternoon and created a diversion by getting free and charging at full gallop into the open french window of the house.

The Sunday school teacher went round with a cake that she had baked herself, inducing people to guess the weight at two pence a time. She asked Jack, the bachelor shepherd, if he would like to try and in clear large print for everyone to see, he wrote just one word, 'Heavy!'

When, by some odd fluke, she won the bowl-off for the pig, however, he volunteered to look after it for her and gave the gossips enough ammunition to last them through to Michaelmas.

The greasy pole was fun. Three poles firmly fixed like a football goal were plastered with cart grease and in the 'All-comers, knock-out contest' each contestant, armed with a sack of straw, had to climb to the other side using the sack to dislodge his opponent en route.

In the tug-of-war, where the vicar's and the farmer's teams fought their yearly battle, everyone felt the vicar's side to be the underdogs and at some disadvantage.

The farmer's team knew there was a stone jug behind the cedar tree and that it contained something that would give them strength, while the vicar's team pulled faces over their sour lemonade.

While the farmer urged his team along in language they could understand, the vicar's supplications were of the 'Pull chaps, pull' calibre.

The evening wore on and as dusk fell the trees around the lawn were magically transformed with coloured lights.

From the verandah, the old gramophone blared tinnily for the couples dancing on the lawn. The bandsmen were free to mingle with girls who had made sheep's eyes at them all the afternoon.

Among the deserted tents, Dad and my brother loaded

crockery and chairs into the wagon and, tucked up on a pile of old curtains, my Whitsun dress all stained and anything but white, I rode down the vicarage drive.

The music of the *Destiny Waltz* still drifted through the trees and pervading it all was the scent of lilac and bruised grass.

Post Hole Willy

Post-Hole-Willy used to live in a stone-built cottage at the far end of Glebe Lane.

Most people in the village called him daft to leave his old home and buy a flimsy new bungalow that was 'nobbut a rabbit hutch on a pocket-hanky plot of land'.

But boyhood memories of his Granny's log fires on the chimney corner hearth wouldn't warm Willy's rheumatics now that he had grown old.

Although he had long since hidden the smoky old fireplace behind an aggressively ugly tiled surround and plaster boarded the solid stone inner walls, rising damp still turned his best boots mildew green, while slugs and snails left slime trails on the mat inside the door.

Daft or not, Post-Hole-Willy sold Stone Cottage, bought his bungalow and still made money on the deal.

There have always been two schools of thought as to whether he is 'a Ha'penny short of a shilling' in the head.

I know that behind the stolid, slow witted face he shows

the world, there's a crafty old schemer with a goblin sense of fun that first earned him his name.

Years ago he came back from the Army, toothless, unmarried and boasting a small pension, a sitting bird for our widowed distant cousin, May.

They married and thereafter Cousin May wept public copious tears, bewailing the loss of her much-lamented first.

Having bought a wife, Willy bought some second-hand teeth, strictly a social asset, too precious to eat with and removed in times of stress.

Strangers being introduced sometimes shook a hand that clutched a still-warm upper denture.

Family pressure forced Dad to find Willy employment on the farm. Hedging, ditching and fencing were safe winter jobs where no-one could go wrong. Willy did his best.

Enthusiastically burning clippings from a hedge that he had just trimmed, he set fire to the hedge.

He fell face first into a deep mud-filled ditch and the fence posts he erected blew down in a breeze. He tried again but the posts still leaned like drunken sailors on a rolling deck.

The milk of Dad's forbearance became skimmed.

"Will", he said. "You didn't get the post holes right".

"Post holes?" asked Willy. "What be they?"

Temptation leered and Dad, no saint, replied, "If you don't know, take the wheelbarrow over to the hurdle maker and ask him for a barrow-load of post-holes."

Smiling cheerfully through his china teeth, Willy wheeled the wooden barrow five miles up and down the lanes.

The perplexed hurdle-maker scratched, thought, then asked which sort of holes Dad wanted, round or square?

This floored Willy's powers of reasoning. He knew there was something about square pegs in round holes but, to be on the safe side, trundled his barrow back to ask Dad.

"Round ones Willy, you're using round posts!" Willy set off back on his third five-mile trip.

The hurdle maker, solemn faced, said,

MARTIN LAW.

"Round ones, eh? Did Harry say what length?"

"Blogger me," said Willy, flagging now. "I ain't going back and from again. Give us a load of whatever size you've got."

Half-past nine, pitch crow's-wing dark and Cousin May a-hammering on the door.

"You mean to say you've sent poor little Willy for a barrow-load of holes?"

"Round ones," said Dad, as if that helped. Ruffled, she squawked and clucked like a broody hen. She'd had one husband slip the net and if Willy wasn't much, he kept her warm at night.

The gate hinge creaked and Willy, a trifle short on wind, came limping to the door.

"Here, boss, those post-holes be blamed airy-fairy things."

Not a glimmer of a smile showed on Willy's face.

"They'd have been terrible awkward to stack on the barrow, so I caught the afternoon bus at the woodyard and went to the agricultural merchants in the town. They said they'd charge it to your account."

Already hovering in the red in the balance at the bank, Dad asked Willy what on earth he'd bought.

"Well, first, the wheel of the barrow has run so far and so fast it was nigh on bursting into flames, so I bought half a gallon of cart grease and a half-hundred-weight of binder twine."

"Binder twine?" Dad was stuck for words.

"That's right. I took it back and tied the start of one ball to the hurdle maker's gate, knotted the end of each ball to the start of the next, and threaded the twine through all they old holes. You'll find any that dropped off the barrow when you collects up all that string."

A wasted day, four hours overtime, cart grease and a half-hundred-weight of cats-cradled useless twine, all for a barrow load of holes. We never did decide just who fooled whom.

Soon after, Post-Hole-Willy as he now became, set himself up as a handyman, and had the Trades Descriptions Act then

POST HOLE WILLY

been in force Willy would have been on shaky legal ground, for everything that he put up fell down.

Sweet smell of revenge

The feud between my father and The Admiral's Niece began one Speech Day at our village school.

The wooden partition dividing the two class-rooms had been propped back and the 'top class' desks, pushed together in three rows, were covered with a strip of thin coco-matting to make an improvised platform at one end of the schoolroom.

On this a group of familiar figures, crammed close together on chairs brought over from the schoolmaster's house, strove to appear dignified as they avoided putting their heels in still-full inkwells or lost their balance as a chair leg slipped into the gaps between the rickety old desks.

The schoolmaster, centre-stage, had exchanged his egg and gravy bespattered woolly waistcoat for a mildewed cap and gown, but his assistant teacher wife still sported two drab 'cardies' and kipper-box, polish-starved boots.

Beside her sat the vicar, beaming beatifically, baby-pink and shiny-faced, as if his most recent occupation had been an

THE SWEET SMELL OF REVENGE

attempt to boil himself in a bath.

His Lordship's steward was there, deputising for 'His Nibs', and not obviously overjoyed at the prospect of an afternoon in a hot, ill-ventilated schoolroom, facing a group of grubby children who were probably laying odds on how soon he would nod off to sleep.

A prosperous fruit-grower, ram-rod straight, sat glaring down. With the apple scrumping season just ahead he seemed to be imprinting a picture of our individual faces in his mind.

In an aura of parma violet scent, and the feather from her hat probing the schoolmaster's left ear, sat The Admiral's Niece.

'Uncle, the Admiral', was a shadowy figure, long deceased, but his niece still set the standards of social niceties as far as local society was concerned.

And right on the end of the platform, with his bowler hat on his knee, sat my Dad, smart in his Harris tweed suit and his shining Sunday boots. All Mum's efforts to get the studs into his starched shirt front and his tie tucked under his stiff collar had been worth it.

Like King George V he looked, only smarter.

I prayed that his pink-painted bedroom chair wouldn't slip off the edge of the stage, and that he would remember the words for his vote of thanks.

On a card table, covered by a Union Jack, was a bunch of flowers in a painted pickle jar, a pile of essays and some books. These I had an interest in, for one could soon belong to me.

The Admiral's Niece, who was to present the prizes, gave an essay award each year and, possibly because I was the only one to write on two sides of a piece of school paper, my effort on 'Why I Want To Join The Navy' had gained the highest mark.

A bumble bee, trapped in the shut windows above the stage, disturbed the dancing dust motes and filled a vacuum of boredom as the speeches droned on.

Unmindful of a deep contralto voice offering advice to

'Those about to leave', I watched the bee until I noticed Dad's right foot tapping in irritation, a storm signal usually reserved for the fools who forgot to shut field gates, or my older sisters when they came home late.

Then the gist of the speaker's remarks filtered through the cobwebs of my mind.

"Low-born country children that you are, do not be dismayed."

The Admiral's Niece's impassioned tones washed over us in waves. "No one among you need go unemployed. There is always domestic service for the girls, and the most simple idiot among the boys could work on the land."

The fruit-grower turned an apoplectic shade of mauve and as Dad stood up to give his vote of thanks, I knew from his tapping foot that practising his set speech had been a sheer waste of time.

"Madam," he began, "the countryside does not necessarily breed fools, nor does noble birth preclude bigotry and patronising condescension."

We may not have understood the long words, but we knew that the Admiral's Niece was not amused. When she reminded Dad that he was not addressing a dairy maid, her face turned crab-apple sour as he replied:

"I realise this, Madam, for I do not believe that you could milk a cow."

The schoolmaster studied the coco-matting between his feet and the vicar, tilting backward in his chair, looked as if he might be praying for the imprisoned bee.

Nevertheless, Speech Day continued and a small procession of prize-winners, undecided whether to bow or curtsey, bobbed across the stage.

The Admiral's Niece held my essay, 'Why I Want To Join The Navy', in her hand, offered some constructive criticism on it and said,

"Now who is entrant number nine?"

I knew, so did the schoolmaster, but as she consulted his

list, The Admiral's Niece gave me one long withering look, extended a glacial gaze in Dad's direction and announced that she had been reading the number upside down. The winner was, in fact, entrant number six.

A surprised lad, who never dreamed that three lines and a page of blots could rate a literary award, ploughed through sardine-packed children to collect his prize. I did not covet his volume of 'Selected Sermons On Sectarianism' any more than I had really wanted to embark on a sea-going career.

The sea was the stuff that Sunday-school treats were made of.

There was always the farmyard pond and a fleet of sheep-troughs to sail from tadpole time until the leaves of the poplars carpeted the surface of the pond.

Prize-giving and the school day over, it was to the solitude of the pond that I escaped. A sheep-trough punt, clothes-line prop propelled, is, strictly speaking, a one-man craft, but I was always prepared to carry passengers for trips around the pond. Customers were few, however, because their mothers seemed to be averse to their offspring going home with slimy, water-stained clothing or pond weed in their hair.

As far as Dad was concerned, the incidents at Speech Day were finished with and, if I had been unfairly treated, the injustices of life were facts that I would have to learn to face. Meanwhile there was a clover crop to cut and carry while the weather held.

Day followed sun-baked day. The pond grew steadily more shallow until it would have been possible to paddle from side to side, had not the bottom been knee deep in evil-smelling mud. The hot weather affected Mum's laying hens, but if egg production had fallen off, the customers to buy them had rapidly diminished since the Speech Day episode.

Spitefulness over a paltry prize was one thing; depriving Mum of her egg money was another. This time Dad would do more than tap his foot.

If we hoped for rain it was not only to save the parched

crops, but because The Admiral's Niece was holding a garden party for her social equals. None of the local ladies was invited, a fact that made one disgruntled lady renew her order for butter and eggs from Mum, despite the displeasure that The Admiral's Niece would show.

The pond had never been so low, an ideal time, Dad said, to clean it out. It stank to high heaven and even Jack, whose personal hygiene left more than a little to be desired, since he never reckoned to wash, complained that "Her didn't 'alf 'um," as he shovelled semi-solid sludge into a dilapidated tip-cart.

The task was finished by mid-afternoon, Dad hitched Phyl, the old half-blind mare, to the shafts and led her slowly out of the farm gate.

"Near side wheel looks a bit dodgy, Harry," Jack called as Dad set out along the lane.

"It will get there if I take it easy," Dad replied.

Half an hour later and he was back, leading Phyl but without a cart.

"I can't understand it. I must have clipped the verge just outside The Admiral's Niece's garden wall, and the rim of the wheel fell off. Old Humph reckons that it will be tomorrow afternoon before he can get it repaired. The hot weather shrank the wood.

"As you say Jack, that pond mud don't half hum and there is that poor lady with all her guests just over the wall."

Dad grinned a little, then, straight-faced, said no-one could move a cart with a broken wheel.

Ballet
equestrienne

Daisy Hackett said that if I held my ear close to the telephone post I would hear messages passing overhead, but no matter how I tried the only sound I heard was the wind in the wires.

Not for me the chance to eavesdrop on the parson pleading for his unrequited love. Daisy Hackett professed to hear it all.

"He says he loves her worse'un toothache!"

"Who?" we asked, intrigued.

"Listen and find out," was all that Daisy would divulge.

"Oo-err!" The other children, crossing their hearts and hoping to die, swore that they could hear the conversation too. Unenlightened, I came to the conclusion that I had been born with the wrong-shaped ears.

It bothered me and I was not sorry when Alfie Hart, riding his father's bike, called out that the self-binder had almost finished cutting winter wheat up on Foxley Bank. The other children ran up there to watch the sport.

Much as I liked rabbit or hare pie, I hated those last few

circuits of cutting a cornfield. As the standing corn grew less any animals or injured game instinctively sought sanctuary towards the centre of the field and when that shelter disappeared they broke cover or crouched, petrified with fear. 'Guns' stood on one side and anyone nimble enough to chase the terrified rabbits waited on the other.

With the others running ahead, I pondered on the problem of my ears, convinced that they were in some way deformed.

I knew that they were perpetually forced forward by the scalp-tight braided plaits in which my mother endeavoured to contain my slippery 'mouse-coat' hair, but an intensive study of my shadow gave no clue as to where the fault might lie.

It perplexed me until I realised that the slim telephone post in School Lane carried only two insulating cups and four thin wires. Ears as misshapen as mine would probably need a larger post to listen-in. The thick one on the corner of Plough Lane should be just right.

It smelled of sun-soaked pine forests and creosote. A resinous gum exuded from its cracks, but I still heard nothing but a vibrating low-pitched hum. With both arms encircling the post, my fingers explored the outline of a notice on the side. That, I reasoned, could easily prevent any telephone conversation from coming down the post.

The poster made enthralling reading. 'Grand Circus and Menagerie. See Titania and her Ballet Equestrienne; Alfredo the Fearless; Wild Beasts of the Jungle. Admission from sixpence up.' The illustration showed Titania as a dainty ethereal creature far removed from our clod-hopping country ways.

Cloistered and enclosed in the stuffy school-room on the following day, we heard rumbling wheels and a traction engine travelling through the village at the top end of School Lane. Alfie Hart, tallest in the class, could just see out of the bottom panes of the school-room window had he dared to look, but he was sitting cowering under the schoolmaster's glacial stare.

"Reckon it was threshing tackle or the steam plough,"

Alfie said at playtime.

"Wasn't then," I argued, smug and feeling smart as paint. "It was the circus moving into town."

They asked me how I knew.

"I found out while I was listening to the telephone post," I said.

"Now let Daisy Hackett pretend she heard the parson talking sloppy to Miss Ash!"

It would be hard to imagine anyone less likely to inflame male passion than Miss Ash. She was a shrewish little woman with halitosis, a permanent digestion problem and an aversion to soap and water. As the village organist and teacher of pianoforte, she suffered from the added disadvantage of being disastrously tone-deaf.

She coached my 'brainy' sister through 'Ezra Read's Easy Tutor' for one hour every week. Mum, full of maternal pride, would stand enraptured as my sister plodded painfully through *The Maiden's Prayer, The Robin's Return* and the *Blue Danube Waltz,* punctuated by off-key promptings and attacks of wind.

There was no music lesson for anyone on the afternoon that we heard the circus lorries pass through.

When I got home from school Miss Ash, looking dustier and more dishevelled than ever, was having hysterics in the kitchen, pausing only to draw breath and swallow down great gulps of Elderberry Wine, Mum's standard medicine for bringing back colour to one's cheeks.

"To be confronted by a lewd looking little man in a loin cloth in the lane was bad enough," she sobbed, "but when I saw that he was actually encouraging a great brute elephant to steal apples from the trees, I poked the pair of them with my gamp, but the wretched beast picked up a trunkful of dust from the wide of the road and blew it in my face!"

Another glass of medicine disappeared, she stopped for a quick scream and was off again.

"One does not expect to meet a wagon load of monkeys

displaying their disgusting habits and believe me or believe me not, they all had blue behinds! It is just not safe for a decent, respectable person to venture forth alone!"

Appalled at the prospect of hours of Miss Ash, I volunteered to walk her home across the fields.

Swaying slightly and slurred of speech, she imagined that lustful men lurked behind every hedge and was so relieved to reach her house intact that she gave me a shilling and promised to show me how to play Chopsticks on the piano when next it was safe to call.

Anything as exotic as a circus was an extremely rare occurrence. I had never been to one before, but nothing was allowed to interfere with harvesting and if I went I would have to go there by myself.

Dad gave me sixpence, three weeks' pocket money in one go. This, with the shilling I had saved, gave me one and six.

Doing a mathematical calculation on the dust of the barn floor, I figured that two fourpenny bus fares, plus the sixpence admission, would leave me with four pennies to spare. It felt wonderful to be rich.

The circus looked much less glamorous than I had imagined it would be. The Big Top had more patches in its canvas than our stack cover tarpaulins at home. Nevertheless, there was a long queue waiting for entry and a long wait before I could say, "A sixpenny ticket, please."

"You're in the wrong queue young'un, menagerie tickets is around the back."

I argued but there it was in black and white.

'Menagerie sixpence, Circus seats from one and six'.

So the menagerie it had to be. Disillusion was complete.

A moth-eaten old lion, a group of dejected monkeys — Miss Ash was right, they did have blue behinds — an elephant with eye trouble and both fore and hind legs hobbled with chains, and two skinny skewbald horses, standing on less straw than my brother would have put in his rabbit hutch.

A man with leopard skin trousers came into the tent,

43

followed by a frowsty woman dressed in trailing tulle and tarnished tinsel.

"Right then Alf, let's get them harnessed," she said, then led the horses out.

"And now, the great Titania!"

The ringmaster's voice carried through the canvas walls of the Big Top. I left the menagerie tent and walked the five miles home.

If that fat woman could be 'Titania, the ballet dancer on a horse', then so could I. I would use the old net curtains that kept the birds from the blackcurrant bushes for a dress and ride Jim, the horse that was the same age as myself. He had an even temper and a broad back.

Privacy was essential for the first few practice rides and since Sunday was the only day that he was turned out to graze, I skipped Sunday school and led him down to the far corner of his meadow by the elms. Draped in blackcurrant stained net, with Jim wearing ploughing reins on his halter, I got up on his back.

Riding Jim was nothing unusual, but he took objection to the hobnails in my Sunday shoes on his bare back and made straight for the low branches of the elms. That is where I stayed.

As Dad said as he extricated me from yards of hampering net hooked up in the tree, few are blessed with beauty, artistry and poise.

The rest of us must work.

Sunday school treat

Chapel children, night clothes clad, stare enviously from upstairs windows in the village street, crying or jeering at us because they cannot come.

We, the children from the church, stand shivering from excitement and the chilling damp of an average summer morning.

Clustered around the open shutters of the gloomy forge we watch the blacksmith bellowing his smouldering hearth into roaring, spark-erupting flames, a foretaste of the fires of hell that the parson warns us of each Sunday in the year.

This year we are safe, for we have been to Sunday school and service frequently enough to gain reprieve. The fact that we are congregating by the forge is proof that we who stand and wait have all been good. No back-sliders are allowed to come!

We hear the chugging engine of the Flying Dutchman's bus, (Daily services to outlying districts. Outings and tours a specialty). The bulbous, brown, solid-tyred charabanc comes

45

rattling up the village street.

Rough boys and older girls jostle and push, rushing to claim the back seat first and get a longer ride. The vicar counts our heads; "Three to a seat, and all sit down!" He tells the Flying Dutchman to proceed, for "All are safely gathered in." At last we are on our way.

My gentle sister, first one from our parts to win a scholarship for more than a decade, has taught the slower children how to say their prayers, so qualifying to sit beside the Sunday school teacher up in front. It makes me proud to think she rates a seat all to herself.

I have found a perch halfway down the bus, wedged between plump Emmy and her flesh-encumbered Mum. Emmy gets 'poorly' if she can't sit by the window, while her Mum's fat overflows the edge of the seat, and I sit sandwiched in between.

"Emmy, here's the dripping toast you didn't eat before we left."

Emmy munches her late breakfast, visibly and audibly enjoying every bite while we rush by the fields of standing corn at a breakneck twenty knots, down one hill, gathering speed to take the hump-backed, tummy-dropping bridge, and charge on up the other side, changing down through the gearbox, gradually losing speed, shuddering, juddering. Clutch is engaged and 'Clunk!' the Flying Dutchman finds his bottom gear. The heavy-laden bus crawls slowly on and up.

Meanwhile Emmy's face has gone an interesting green; it happens every year!

"You'll have to stop, my Emmy isn't well."

The Flying Dutchman knows that if he does, he'll never start again and, posing deaf, drives on.

My string-handled, paper carrier bag that advertises Mr. Brown's wet and dry fish is hauled up from the danger zone and my new seaside bucket is sacrificed to the cause.

At the top of the hill, the other children cheer because the sea is in sight. My vision is restricted to the ham-like arms of

Emmy's Mum, mopping up her bucket-clutching child.

Down the hill and through the little seaside town, until we stop and unpack, like sardines walking from their tin.

A cold and drizzling wind is blowing off the sea. Emmy's Mum says "Thanks" and ceremoniously hands me back my half-full bucket, advising me to rinse it in the sea. The tide is out and half a mile away, but I trudge out across the shingle beach until I reach the waves and, all alone, imagine that there is nothing in the world but sea, the lowering clouds and me.

Salt splashing in my best brown button boots, I run like mad to find my sister and my friends; there's nothing more scarifying than the thought of being lost in a strange town.

Emmy, fully recovered, is on the swing boats, eating chips from a paper bag.

It is far too cold to linger on the front and, safe with my sister, we cross the esplanade and go across into Penny Arcade. We use up all our pennies, save the two that Mum says we must always keep 'in case', then watch the tall boys, laughing, holding up their shorter friends, trying to cram four eyes into the visor meant for two, to find out for themselves just what it was that the butler saw.

Across the sea, a line of blue marks a break in the clouds. It is going to clear up. The sun comes out and like lemmings we are drawn toward the sea.

Removing boots and socks, we younger girls tuck petticoats and dresses in our knicks, screaming as the cold waves creep between our toes, while braver ones walk out in the water, right up to their knees!

One or two, who go to the seaside more than one day in the year, have gone to the extreme of wearing swimming suits; with chattering teeth and blue-faced with cold, they say it's lovely when you're in!

My sister, neither child enough to tuck her skirts up in her pants, nor old enough to join the vicar and his wife drinking coffee in the Grand Cafe, envies us our paddle.

The intelligence that gained her a higher education overcomes the problem and works out the way for her to have a dip. I must stay on the beach, while she goes off towards the council bathing station. Some good few sea-wasting minutes and she is back, tripping like Aphrodite to the sea, clad in a yellow stockinette swimming costume, two sizes too large and boldly printed right across the rear, 'Property of the Urban District Council'.

The sun has sulked again, so in a large glass-fronted shelter we eat jam sandwiches for lunch. Conscious of a debt of gratitude, Emmy's Mum shares a pint of winkles with us, taking the 'gob-stopper' hatpin from her head to show me how to get them out. This time the bucket comes in handy for the shells.

It settles in for rain and doubting disbelief runs riot in my soul. Surely the Lord could let the sun shine on this one day in the year. Was it for this we went to Sunday school in ice and snow? For this we stamped our chilblained feet in a draughty, cold church hall, consoling ourselves that it was all worth while to be allowed to go to the summer seaside treat?

Death, heaven and hell are a million years away, the seaside is here and now! It seems the obvious time for Deity to signify He knows that we have tried. And then He lets it rain!

My sister calms down my rebellious spirit and lets me try to catch six ping-pong balls in a shrimping net. A boy beside me catches five from the fountain jet of water; the man in charge takes his hand off the button, the water subsides and the balls disappear. We protest, volubly and at length, that it is a swindle and my sister, education bent, takes me off to see the town museum. 'Closed for lunch, open at 2.30 p.m.'

Back past The Gem Cinema, its placards boasting 'Come inside and see what France is really like!' My sister can speak French, which astounds us who find it hard to write and spell our native tongue. She would like to know more about France so, screwing up her long hair in a bun and looking worried, in the hope it makes her look sixteen, she buys 'One nine-penny and a half.'

The dim light of a tiny torch pilots us through the Stygian darkness to sit in the front row. At least it is warm and dry in here.

France seems to be a dreadful sort of place, where the nicest thing that happens to a sweetly pretty girl is that she is dipped in wax and ends up as a statue. Her friend is carried screaming to a boat that's bound for South America. It says so underneath!

I can't see why she is making such a fuss, the gentlemen around her seem so friendly, but my sister says it is far worse than being dipped in boiling grease.

The Blue Grotto Cafe is the venue for our Sunday school tea, curled-up, dry cucumber sandwiches and lovely creamy sticky cakes.

Emmy, full to the teeth, regards the last cake on the plate and with ladylike delicacy, wraps it in her paper serviette and puts it up her knicker leg, to eat on the way home.

There is an hour to kill before we can depart and in the bay a cargo ship is heading for the harbour. The vicar suggests that we might like to go and see it dock.

My sister is reluctant to go. The film this afternoon showed what could happen to a girl who wanders near sea-going ships. Mum would be cross if we did that, then woke up bound for Buenos Aires.

The welcome, familiar bus is just across the road and 'everyone will please remember where they sat before'. I hope that someone forgets but fate decrees that, once again, I act as buffer state between fat Emmy and her Mum.

Knowing too well that once we reach the hump-backed bridge and start to climb the hill on the other side, Emmy will start to bawl and be sick again, I take Dad's stick of rock and Mum's giant peppermint humbug from my bucket and pass it on to Emmy, now engrossed in her squashed, sat-upon cake.

It is quite a job to lift my leaden-weighted lids. Perhaps I'll

49

go to sleep till we get home. Tomorrow I must start another year, laying up treasure in heaven and making sure I qualify to go on next year's Sunday school outing to the sea.

Harvest
bunfight

Lockley Harvest Gala is one of the few remaining threads from a pattern of living as remote now as the rural world of Jethro Tull.

In a working year not overblessed with festive occasions Lockley Harvest Sports and Supper, otherwise known as 'His Lordship's Bunfight', brought a bonus work-free Saturday to each autumn.

It was a long walk from our village, but no-one willingly missed 'the Bunfight', since it gave us the opportunity to glimpse life as it was lived behind the high walls surrounding Lockley Park, His Lordship's country seat.

The main entrance was on the other side of the estate but at 10.20. precisely on 'Bun-fight' morning an under game-keeper unlocked the huge iron gates at the bottom of Lockley Hill. We trooped in and along the tree-lined, mile-long drive.

Children from Lockley School and ours, segregated from their parents, washed and inspected behind the ears, waited in subdued lines as their school teachers briefed them yet

51

again.

It was forbidden to damage the turf, pick any flowers or fruit or be 'excused' behind a tree. There must be no staring at the statues. These, it was explained, were Art, portraying heathen gods and therefore of no interest to us.

Aphrodite, Adonis, Circe, Ceres, Juno and Saturn were consequently studied in great depth, providing the first instruction in basic anatomy to every goggle-eyed child. Two-headed Janus, damaged by a misplaced shot at a low-flying pheasant, had lost a chunk of his marble. The uneducated tenantry knew him as 'Old Minus', whether they could read the writing on his plinth or not.

No child must behave boisterously and should 'Young Master Frederick', known to his contempories as 'Right Horrible Fred', compete in any race, he must not be jostled or pushed. As His Lordship's heir he would naturally win.

Otherwise, the youngsters were free to enjoy themselves before their own races began by watching a twenty-over cricket match between His Lordship's XI and the Farmers' team.

Since all the inhabitants of Lockley village and a good percentage of our own were tenants of the estate, His Lordship's side comprised the best cricketers from both communities, plus any house guests — 'London folk' to us.

The Farmers' scratch team seldom won when the bowlers dutifully avoided His Lordship's stumps and the fielders felt obliged to drop each catch.

While the cricket match was in progress, the womenfolk and smaller children gathered near the yew arches that screened the back terrace lawns.

Her Ladyship, her female guests and the Lockley district nurse came out through the conservatory doors and down the terrace steps. Infants were hauled from their prams and toddlers had their faces 'quick-licked' clean. The nurse jostled the mothers into groups, according to their offspring's age.

Her Ladyship progressed along the ranks, pinching cheeks,

admiring clothing. Showing the correct amount of indecision, she chose the best and bonniest baby in each group. It was immaterial that the chosen child was so bloated that it suffered from croup for nine months of the year.

Weight was the deciding factor, just as prize winning porkers or spring lambs were adjudged to be those that gained the most poundage in the shortest time. Her Ladyship's criterion of a healthy baby was much the same.

A snack lunch was served between the two innings of the cricket match, but by then the school children who had sat still for so long were wriggling and remembering that they were forbidden to 'go behind a bush'. Not that they would voluntarily have done so, for using the gardening staff's 'offices' was a highlight of the day.

When most of our homes lacked piped water and had wooden privies 'out the back', the tiled walls, polished mahogany seats and gleaming white porcelain bowls were a source of admiration.

To tug a chain and unleash 'The Niagara (Patent Pending)', was both exhilerating and terrifying as the rushing water flushed and gurgled in the cistern overhead. It was an experience to savour as often as one dared.

With the cricket charade over for another year, the children's races could begin. Three-legged, sacked, egged, spooned and hampered by their Sunday clothes, each tried to outrace the others, ever mindful that if 'Right Horrible Fred' took part, then he must set the pace.

Each competitor was rewarded with a toffee-apple, usually a windfall Worcester shrivelling in a rock-hard burnt sugar shroud.

The men's events provided much more fun, with local rivalries emerging and each participant determined to take home any livestock that was going free. Climbing the greasy pole faster than anyone else meant a weaner pig from the home farm to fatten for Christmas in one's garden sty. Tossing the tree trunk, heaving the hammer, tilting the bucket —

each contestant stood the chance of winning a young cockerel or laying hen. Then the obstacle races, scrambling under stack covers, over pig nets, through swinging barrels and a sluggish flowing stream.

The athletic activities culminated in the tug-of-war, Lockley team against our own. This was the most partisan contest of them all, since a guinea and a cask of cider were at stake.

Eight men from each village, taking the strain on a four-inch rope, dug the heels of their Sunday boots into the resilient turf, undid their collar studs and, eye-balls protruding, heaved.

By now the electric lights in the glass covered coach-house yard beckoned our attention. It was time for the annual Harvest tea. Sheaves of corn and mop-headed chrysanths decorated the wrought iron uprights supporting the glass roof, flags of the empire decorated the walls, and bodies crammed together to get seated round the trestle tables on which the feast was set.

'Right Horrible Fred' presided at the children's table, liberally spattering his guests with remnants of the pink blanc-mange rabbits that crouched on green jelly grass.

The grown-ups tackled a much more substantial meal, which everyone was expected to help in clearing away. This gave the more inquisitive a chance to see the cavernous back kitchens of the 'big house'.

'Order for His Lordship'. Mouse quiet, we listened to his usual annual speech, gave three cheers for the king, the estate, and a good harvest and then began to sing.

His Lordship always started with *The Farmer's Boy,* and we dutifully sang the choruses. For several years a singer, announced as being Lady Cordite, warbled *Cherry Ripe* or *Lo Hear The Gentle Lark.* Having acknowledged the applause, this individual would reveal himself as the estate secretary in 'drag'.

Children who had never seen a wig were impressed, their elders muttered that 'Yonder chap were summat odd'.

HARVEST BUNFIGHT

When a genuine contralto gave a recital of German lieder, our response was cool indeed as we sat waiting for her to remove her hair and gown.

We came out onto the familiar lane at the bottom of Lockley Hill and went our separate ways home.

Distinctly feudal, definitely homespun, His Lordship's Bunfight produced enjoyment and spontaneous laughter. It generated a humorous vitality that, despite the 'star attractions' displays and sophisticated side-shows, the efficiently run present-day Gala lacks.

Rabbit
stew

That season had been a never-ending series of disasters and, not to put too fine a point on it, we were broke. Late frosts had halved our fruit crop, the season's hay had gone up in a stack fire and, as a finale to the summer, an outbreak of swine fever plunged the bank balance down below the thin red line.

True, the yield from the hard-won harvest was still an unknown quantity. That would stay in the barn until we were solvent enough to get it threshed, but Dad would borrow from no one. What he could not pay for we would not have.

We were rich, he said, in everything but money and if there was no cash in the kitty there was no need for us to starve.

Economy would be our password and we would build up our resources in any legal manner we could. These then were the circumstances that led to what for me will always be the days of rabbit stew.

Not that butcher's meat had ever been a frequent feature on our menus. In more affluent times there had always been

56

MARTIN LAW.

a fattened pig to provide meat for the winter, but now the sties were empty and burying swine fever victims in quick-lime had killed our taste for pork. Previously we often had a Sunday chicken dinner, but now every egg layer counted and if one found its way into the pot it was some egg-bound old boiler, 'killed to stop it dying', as my mother used to say.

In those pre-myxomatosis days it fell to the ubiquitous bunny to provide the mainstay of our meals and should any-one ever feel inspired to compile and publish a 'Hundred and One Things to do with your Rabbit,' I could contribute to every page.

We ate them stewed, we ate them roasted, boiled with dumplings, frittered, fried and battered, 'rabbit in the hole' or rabbit pasties and a thick pastry lid covered many a 'mystery' pie.

That was not always one hundred per cent rabbit, but who were we to argue if some suicidal pheasant chose to end it all by putting its neck in the noose of a snare.

We had a gentleman's agreement not to poach the squire's pheasants, but if the squire was a gentleman I knew his son was not. That, to my way of thinking, made the whole thing null and void. One of the estate gamekeepers who often used to drop in at mealtimes knew how we were situated and would compliment Mum or me on our 'feathered rabbit' pie.

Earlier in the year I had found an injured tame rabbit by the roadside. I took it home and within a fortnight there were eight. Each had a name, they grew fat and flourished, then all but one were sold to swell our funds. Mum said that there would be no wild rabbit for that year's Boxing Day dinner, we would eat the remaining tame rabbit instead. It was just like being asked to sit down and enjoy a meal made from one of the friendly farmhouse cats.

Even when it was nothing but stock and stewed bones, its pelt, scraped, salted and treated with alum hung in reproach-ful accusation, curing and nailed up on a board.

Later Mum would use it to line mittens, ideal for cold

winter working on the farm.

As the cook book says, first catch your rabbit and if ever there were double standards on a subject this was it. The dear little flopsy, cotton-tail, story-book bunny close-cropped pasture, decimated young corn crops and chewed his way through the shoots of growing trees. It was the country-side's most ravenous nuisance, yet to catch a rabbit was not regarded as pest destruction but poaching, on any land one neither hired or owned.

Some of our farms were badly affected for, although it was our crops that they cleared, the actual rabbit warrens were mostly just inside the squire's woods on the other side of the hedge. There were often dozens of rabbits grazing and with the asking rate at a shilling a rabbit from the butcher, this seemed a source of income worthy of being explored.

The saddler sold rabbit snares unofficially and Slippy Springer the poacher watched with interest as I bought mine. "Setting up in opposition then, girl?" he enquired then, walking home beside me, gave a discourse on his art. A good poacher, according to Slippy, was one who ran quicker and thought faster than his opponents.

He offered to set my snares out for me and soon there were hingles, as he called them, set out in every rabbit track in Stony Field.

"You won't catch much tonight but you should do better the night after," he warned me. "You want to walk round them about half an hour after the rise of the sun."

I couldn't sleep for thinking of dead rabbits and was up and over in Stony Field before it was really light. By the time I was half-way round I had found thirty rabbits, far too many to carry in my bag.

I saw some movement in the hedge in the field's far corner, and there was Slippy carrying an empty sack. He looked surprised to see me, then grinned and helped me carry my rabbit catch home.

"You know something?" he said as he puffed along beside

me, "I reckon that besides running and thinking faster, I'd better add getting up earlier to my list."

On a fifty-fifty basis, Slippy volunteered to use his ferrets to clear the burrows on our land. Sometimes the ferrets would 'lay-up' with a dead rabbit and, full-tummied, would go to sleep underground. There was nothing for it then but to sit and wait if the project was legal, otherwise one cut one's losses and ran.

While I had been a part-time rabbit catcher, Mum had been engaged on her profit-making scheme. In addition to fur-lined mittens she collected every bright piece of cloth she could lay hands on, cut it into strips and hooked it into enormous kitchen rugs. Our clothes line often bore some extremely weird and gaudy garments that Mum had unearthed in some second-hand clothes shop, borne home in triumph and washed. With corn sacks for backing, Mum's bright patterned rugs were virtually indestructible and were snapped up by the hardware store in town.

Scrap iron was sold to gipsies and everything we could produce that had a marketable value was sold. Each pound that we acquired was laboriously entered in an old account book until Dad was able to start using black ink instead of red.

One day, while Mum was serving up the inevitable rabbit stew, she told us that a man had called that morning. He had been out driving and lost his way.

"Such a nice man," Mum had thought him because he had noticed what she was making and had actually purchased a pair of her fur-lined gloves.

When she asked him to step into the kitchen while she wrapped them he offered to give her ten shillings for a pair of ornaments on the kitchen shelf.

"I told him that you would be in within minutes Dad, but he was in a hurry to be off, although he promised to be back."

We looked at Great-aunt Polly's china shepherd and shepherdess with new respect. Tricksters were an alien element in our lives but if the stranger was interested in figurines Dad thought it a worthwhile idea to check up on their value.

Mum and I took them to a reputable antique shop in the town and sold them for more than we dared hope. Now there would be money to pay for threshing the harvest and the price of corn was high.

"We ought to celebrate," said Mum. "Let's buy a pound of steak."

Flanagan's summer

Strangers to the village looked askance to see Flanagan sunning himself in the Post Office window.

But regular customers knew that he kept to the 'official' corner, ignoring the temptations beyond the cards of potmenders, flypapers and sweating cheese that defined the limits of the grocery section.

His unusual black and tan markings saved him from being drowned at birth, thus forfeiting the first of his nine lives.

Life No. 2 and four inches of his tail were lost acquiring the knowledge that a mowing machine moves faster than a half-grown kitten stalking rabbits in a hayfield. The remaining stump of tail sprouted like a fluffy, multicoloured shaving brush in contrast to the rest of his smooth coat.

His tattered ears and scarred eyelids, a legacy from fighting other toms, gave him a wild piratical expression. In fact Flanagan was an extremely ugly cat, but every litter in the vicinity seemed to produce black and tan kittens and the village people recognised him for the character he was.

62

FLANAGAN'S SUMMER

Tom the cowman, whose rough hands could send static electricity tingling through the fur along his spine, was Flanagan's friend, as was the fishmonger who fed him titbits from his reeking, flyblown van. The vicar, who twice yearly pinned a notice on the Post Office door in an effort to find 'good Christian homes for unusual charming kittens', harboured extremely uncharitable thoughts about Flanagan and Flanagan knew it, but realised that the vicar was too gentle to transform words into deeds by way of a well-aimed brick.

The only human who caused Flanagan to arch his back in sheer dislike was a loud-voiced, flat heeled female, who now stood complaining to his mistress that the unhygienic, misbegotten tom-cat should be banned from wandering in the shop. The object of her venom extended and retracted his claws, glanced at her through half-closed eyelids, then darted past her size eight brogues, hurrying towards the fish van that had pulled up in the square.

The same hectoring voice demanded fresh fish for 'the Rose of Sharon, my pedigree Persian Queen', while Flanagan sniffed at the melted packing ice that dripped a slimy trail along the road.

He had no idea what a 'Persian Queen' might be, but he knew there would be good pickings from the unfilleted plaice she was going to eat.

Flanagan followed the hefty brogues until they entered the glass conservatory that served as the side entrance to Rose Villa, and through the glass saw a gorgeous female cat with a silky coat that shone like rain-washed slate. He put back his head and yowled like any farmyard tom, before a size eight brogue dispatched him from the premises with unexpected accuracy.

Nothing daunted, he took cover in the privet hedge and waited for the lovely creature to come out, keeping vigil all day and night without success. But next day, when the flat-heeled shoes pounded past his hiding place, he called to the cat beyond the glass again. She was obviously impressed but

63

stayed inside her prison.

Flanagan knew the 'hard to get routine' and slipped away, returning with a young leveret which he placed beside the door.

The cat inside sniffed and scratched ineffectively, but Flanagan leapt at the latch, throwing the weight of his body against the door until it creaked open and the prisoner was free.

Sharon, born to a world where pedigree breeding was a financial undertaking, raised on a diet of cooked fish and yeast tablets, groomed daily with scented flea powder, was the most unnatural female that Flanagan had ever encountered.

She picked daintily at the strange tasting young hare, then meekly followed Flanagan through the fields of young wheat and into the undergrowth of a wooded valley. There, in the base of a hollow ash tree, Flanagan and Sharon found a place for shelter and warmth.

In a few days Sharon lost her pampered show-cat look, growing sleek and supple.

Flanagan brought food to her and cleaned her coat with his rough tongue until the hunting instincts that generations of careful breeding had submerged stirred again and Sharon hunted beside him. All summer long they ran wild in the woods, stalking food or playing like kittens, chasing dancing leaves.

The £10 reward for the safe return of the valuable 'Rose of Sharon' caused a nine-day wonder that sent every village child prying into ditches and old barns, but no-one worried about Flanagan. He had gone off courting before.

One avid anti-vivisectionist gave her opinion that cat snatchers were abroad but as the village poacher said, his dog ferret had escaped but he didn't accuse anyone of stealing it for laboratory experiments.

The yellowing reward notice faded in the August sun and was forgotten.

FLANAGAN'S SUMMER

Clattering combine harvesters echoed to the valley woods and Flanagan set off to catch the easy prey that huddles limp and lame on the edge of stubbled fields. He hunted alone, for the shimmering heat made Sharon's distended body an intolerable burden and the birth of her kittens was imminent.

The sun had swung across the sky but Sharon had only managed to produce one offspring, while her brain and body concerted together in a cacophony of pain that held her screeching and screaming for relief.

Another creature disturbed the peace of the summer evening and petrified rabbits crouched in their burrows, until the danger passed beyond the range of their senses.

This creamy coloured animal stood on its hind legs to sniff the blood in the air, establishing the direction of its target and insinuated its fluid, undulating body towards Sharon.

The poacher's ferret was out hunting too.

In her agony Sharon was unaware of the danger until the ferret's teeth closed on the helpless kitten and, despite her frantic struggle, the ferret had torn a second kitten from her before merciful blackness engulfed the stricken cat.

Flanagan, dragging a full-grown partridge in his mouth, sensed danger as he struggled through the wood. A jay screamed out a warning and Sharon's last agonised call triggered off the primeval wild cat instinct in her mate.

A spitting, snarling, scratching fury sprang at the satiated ferret, and they writhed in an undefinable mass of flying creamy brown and black and tan fur.

Flanagan felt needle sharp teeth grinding on the bones of his haunches, and as a retaliatory measure, darted talon claws to seek and scratch at the retina of the ferret's unblinking eyes. At last the ferret lay lifeless and in the trees a magpie signalled that the woods were safe again.

Licking his wounds, Flanagan discovered that his hindquarters were lead heavy and not inclined to move. He crawled to Sharon and cleaned her blood-flecked coat, mewing quietly to her until she stirred and tried to rise.

65

Slowly, deliberately, Flanagan took the supine cat by the scruff of her neck and dragged her, kitten-like, down through the woodland and across the stubbled fields, each corn stalk probing and prodding his torn body and useless hindquarters.

It took a night of struggling, resting and struggling on again before Flanagan reached the village. The sun was up before he reached Rose Villa to caterwaul and scratch against the door, with Sharon still cradled gently against him.

The loud-voiced woman, drinking early morning tea, heard the unfamiliar sound and hurried to the door.

"Sharon!" she bellowed, and Tom the cowman, hurrying past on his way to work, was in time to see her slipper-clad foot take a goalkeeper's kick at Flanagan, dispatching him across the sun scorched lawn, to land under the privet hedge.

Tom realised that Sharon needed veterinary help, for years of inbreeding had turned the normal process of birth into a hazardous business and, on the whitened doorstep, delivered her of an abnormally large black and tan kitten.

The woman, stunned to silence by Tom's caustic tongue, found voice again.

"Ruined! It's no good for either showing or breeding now. Get rid of that mongrel kitten, too!"

Tom gathered the cat and kitten in his arms.

"I wasn't reckoning on leaving them here. You'mm too handy with your feet.

"I know where they will be welcomed, but you're too daft to see that old Flanagan had the sense to bring her where she could get help. I heard a commotion in the wood last night and found a darned great ferret lying dead, with enough cat fur around to fill a cushion.

"That old tom cat must have fought like a tiger to save his mate. I wonder where the old rascal is?"

Tom found him lying still and glassy-eyed for, under the dark green dusty hedge where it had begun, Flanagan's summer had ended.

Sheep-dip and home-made wine

Whenever campions bloom, my mind's eye re-creates the sun-soaked summer evening that found our village policeman lying with his helmet over his face and ladies bedstraw twining in his hair, oblivious of his steaming uniform, ruined and reeking of sheep-dip, or of his bicycle lying bent and battered in the stagnant ditch. Wheat-wine bewitched, he simply did not care.

The day had been warm, ideal weather for dipping the recently-sheared sheep.

Sheep-dipping to rid them of parasites and prevent them being maggot-blown by flies was obligatory by law and the police had to be informed when this operation was taking place. This ensured that our guardian of the law would put in an appearance, verify that we were complying with the law, sign the appropriate forms from the Min-of-Ag-and-Fish and then depart.

Since we were a comparatively law-abiding lot — give or take an overlooked dog licence or two and a bit of poaching —

67

our constable was glad to spend the sleepy stillness of a summer afternoon watching lesser men struggle with strong-willed, stubborn sheep that were reluctant to be dipped.

Before insecticides became available we used a dip that was arsenic based, so that when the sheep emerged they looked as if they had been caught in a shower of custard.

The dipping tank was an oblong wooden trough, rather like an oversized bath tub, with a ramp and platform at each end.

The theory was that the sheep would walk up the ramp. There, one of two men would turn it on its back and, with both men holding a leg at each corner and a third man covering its nostrils and mouth, the sheep would be lowered gently into the dip.

But our sheep were distinctly unco-operative and objected to the indignities heaped upon them. Shaking their shorn fleece in disapproval as they stood draining on the second platform, they walked down the ramp, ludicrous comedians mincing along in wet long johns.

Not being hefty enough to handle wet and struggling sheep, I was designated 'sheep's chiropodist', trimming back overgrown hooves with pruning shears and treating any foot ailments with a liberal coat of stockholm tar.

Every village had its reservoir of casual labour, men prepared to help out when extra labour was required. Being a 'one man, one girl' set-up, we often relied on this kind of help.

Although a neighbouring farmer lent a reciprocal hand, our third man at sheep-dipping time was always Jack. Some regarded Jack as a grubby old man who was so mean that he relied on the sheep shearers for his annual haircut, but to him it was simply a matter of priorities.

The other men of the village could do as they chose, but it seemed sheer waste to pay out sixpence to have the squire's groom cut his hair with horse clippers in the 'pent-us' of the blacksmith's shop on Saturday afternoon.

Besides, by having his hair cut once a year at shearing time, it grew long enough to keep the draughts away from his neck in bed all winter long.

Washing, too, folk made too much fuss about.

"Takes all the natural oils out of 'un," Jack maintained, and reckoned that we had much to learn from sheep.

"Look at they. Only bath once a year, and then it's because some Jack-in-an-office says they must. It's certain that they don't get dipped for choice."

Arguing that sheep get washed with rain made no impression.

"Ain't I out in all weathers, too?" was Jack's stock reply, and there was no gainsaying that. Nevertheless, when we went sheep-dipping, we always tried to keep upwind from Jack.

Our constable was always trying to reform Jack to more hygienic ways, so that when they came in contact with each other at our dipping tank, the atmosphere was acrimonious as well as strong. The smell of sheep-dip-saturated clothing that had been on Jack's back for weeks on end was almost unendurable for everyone and it was not by accident that Jack joined the sheep in the tub.

He was convinced that in some way the constable was responsible for his immersion and although Dad offered to stop operations while he got a bucket of warm water and some clean old clothes so that Jack could change, Jack refused and carried on.

The tension eased with the arrival of Mum, carrying a jug of cider and a dusty bottle of home-made, ice-cold wine.

We thought Jack uncommonly sporting to refuse anything but a mug of cider, leaving the policeman to tackle the cool wine.

"Very mild and most refreshing," was his verdict, coming back for another swig.

"I'll go down to the house with your missus Harry, to sign the cattle papers and perhaps she could find another glass of the cold drink."

He was back within a few minutes, looking slightly red

above the dog-collar of his tunic.

And at that moment Jack was preparing to drive Billy, our old ram, up the ramp and on to the platform. With an evading jump, Billy darted out of Jack's grasp, turned smartly on one hoof and charged at the policeman's rear, just as he was approaching the dipping tank.

When he surfaced, brushing sheep's wool and filthy yellow sheep dip from his eyes, he felt around for his helmet and mustering what dignity he could, strode down the yard to the pump, and there with her usual gentle tact, Mum soothed his ruffled pride, sluiced off his tunic and offered him another glass of wine.

Since it was just a cooling, home-made summer drink, he saw no reason to refuse. He came back to the dipping pen to collect his bike surprisingly cheerful considering that his uniform was turning a peculiar shade of green.

Sheep-dipping was finished and everyone but Jack was cleaned up ready for our evening meal when an anxious police-sergeant came to the door.

Our constable should have rendezvoused with him two hours before, and now he was nowhere to be found.

Where the first bend curves down at the top of Lockley Hill the summer flowers fill the banks waist high and there I found him, sleeping in the sun. No-one mentioned Mum's wheat wine, and Jack explained to the sergeant that a sheep-dip bath can have a mighty peculiar effect on folks that wash their 'natural oils' away.

Doris

We had a telephone answering service long before the arrival of automatic exchanges and STD. It was run by Doris, daughter of the postmistress. She alone understood the intricacies of the exchange switchboard in the storeroom of the village Post Office Stores.

Doris knew if the person we were ringing had gone out and where they had gone, where the district nurse was likely to be and why and the wholesale price of brussels sprouts as quoted to Charlie Carter by a city market salesman the previous day.

Few felt the need to have a phone installed when the blue enamelled sign above the store-room door invited everyone to 'Telephone From Here'.

Telephoning was an awesome business. Even Doris addressed the mouthpiece firmly, as if there was an uncontrollable hound tied to the other end of the line. Asking Doris to phone for us dispensed with the need actually to use an instrument that most of us regarded with distrust.

Doris took messages for non-subscribers. The information,

71

'Cousin Albert going to hospital with his leg,' scribbled on blue sugar-bag paper and delivered by children going home from school, was just the bare bones. Doris would relate the meat of the message as soon as one called at the Post Office Stores.

When Doris was off duty her mother acted as stand-in. It was never 'Number, please' or 'Trying to connect you' when Doris's Mum was in charge of the exchange. Instead a voice broad with accent would enquire:

"Who did 'ee want to chat to then?" and knowing, advise the caller to "Just hang on while I puts this-yere plug in that there hole and finds out who we've got."

The crowning achievement for our village exchange was a call from Mrs. Wall's sailor son. He rang from Australia at two o'clock one morning to tell his mother that it was his wedding day and to introduce her to his bride.

The bridegroom's mother, with steel curlers in her hair and wearing a coat over her nightie, stood in the cluttered store-room among the bags of haricot beans and packets of porridge oats, awestruck that Doris was capable of using the wonders of a scientific age to connect her to her son.

Old Dubber Wall, the bridegroom's grandfather, refused to be impressed and voiced doubts in the shop the following day. If Australia was the unnatural sort of place where folks could get married and telephone around the world at the time of night when decent people were in their beds and fast asleep, he was not sure that the tenuous link between Doris's switch-board and the antipodes was entirely a good idea.

Explaining international date lines and time lags was use-less. No-one was going to tell Dubber that if he died eating his breakfast in Britain he could still be alive at teatime in Australia.

Dubber resigned himself to the fact that the silly young shaver had got mixed up with a topsy-turvy parcel of odd folk who didn't know that day is light and night is dark.

"Originals, they call them," said Dubber, quite convinced

that his new grand-daughter would turn out to be some nocturnal being to whom the laws of gravity did not apply.

Doris, queen of the headphones, probably bent every rule in the telephone operator's handbook but she sorted out our problems, saved our twopences and was sometimes instrumental in saving our lives. When a runaway tractor crushed a farmer's son Doris's telephonic tracking service located a doctor on his rounds and got him to the accident within a matter of minutes.

Then Doris dropped a very large stone in the placid pond of our rural existence by divulging that the switchboard in the storeroom would soon be obsolete. The small brick building in the course of erection in the corner of the orchard by the shop was not, as rumour had it, a public convenience. It was the new telephone exchange.

"I am being automated," Doris explained regretfully. Ethel Tappit, spokeswoman, expressed the customers' concern and shock.

"Automated? How disgusting! You don't want to give up so easy, girl. You're not so long in the tooth that some chap won't come along and wed you, decent like. There is always Perce the post. Automated indeed! What will they think of next?"

Indispensable and seemingly as indestructible as a leather coat that gathers a few wrinkles but never seems to age, Perce the village postman was as much a part of the local scene as the mounting steps by the churchyard gate. Having shunned the spinster-spun webs of marriage, his small market garden and his postal round had been his life.

His fruit and vegetables always seemed to flourish and mature weeks ahead of neighbouring gardeners' and Perce reckoned that he knew the reason why.

"I talks to 'em when I'm weeding and hoeing, see! Now if that were a wife she would answer back. Besides, you can't sell your old woman like you can a bunch of carrots."

His Post Office bicycle was his pride and joy, brought out

to be dusted, oiled and have the tyres pumped up each Saturday afternoon, then put back in the shed.

Perce did his postal rounds on a tricycle built like an ordinary cycle with a box car on the side. It was extremely difficult to ride and few children who grew up around here escaped scarred knees from injuries inflicted while attempting to ride and stay on Perce's trike.

The tricycle box carried mail, parcels, greengrocery, odds and ends of shopping orders and anyone with strong nerves requiring a lift.

Perce always started his rounds early so no-one really objected if it was sometimes gone eight o'clock before the mail arrived. We knew that Perce would have lit a fire and got in a day's supply of fuel for the arthritic old lady along School Row, looked in to see that Amos had not had another funny turn and probably delivered a medical prescription to an outlying farm.

If Perce was actually delivering mail he wore his postman's hat. If it was a business or social call he took it off.

Should the two coincide he would first deliver the letter wearing his hat, then remove it while he served the greengrocery order.

There is a gentle incline down Plough Lane. Perce always took advantage of this to sort out his letters as he freewheeled down the middle of the road. When the tricycle was superseded by a small van Perce was too set in his ways to let mechanisation alter his routine.

Local drivers realised that they were liable to be confronted by Perce checking the mail as he drove along Plough Lane. The verge, though wide, bore many tyre ruts from those who had chickened out.

I once had a passenger who abandoned ship as Perce approached. Stopping a good headlight's width away, Perce called out, "Two lettuce or three?"

My somewhat shattered visitor asked if it was a country custom to choose the amount of mail one wanted and commented that it must be highly irregular to carry greengrocery around in an official mail van.

"Ah," said Perce, picking up a bunch of shallots.

"Things is different here to what they be in town. I carry such as these, so that if I get hi-jacked I can stuff these onions up the bandits' nose. Powerful things, onions. Better than tear gas, onions are."

By comparison to the Post Office services our village has known, urban communications seem very tame indeed.

The saga of Florrie Ford

To the true countryman, the land is a living thing to be respected and farmed as if one expected to live for ever. This was the doctrine Harry preached and one that I understood before I was taught to read or write.

School was just for 'book-learning'. Real education came from tending the living land.

Since the basis of good cultivation stems from the ability to use a plough, Harry deemed it necessary to train me in that art. I sat on an upturned bushel basket in the draughty cart-shed, using bath-brick to remove the rust from the brist-board of a plough.

"Keep on polishing, boy, and keep 'un greased and shone."

That this 'boy' was in fact a spindle-shanked, skinny-ribbed girl with plaits made not the slightest difference, I was there to watch an expert 'set' a plough.

Wielding a huge spanner to adjust the coulter that cuts through the soil vertically and the share that slices horizontally beneath the surface of the soil, I tried to get them

properly spaced and lined up with the beam or frame of the plough.

If I had got it right, the furrow would be neither too shallow nor too wide. The brist or mould-board I had polished was fixed to the wide end of the plough share and curved out along the length of the beam, thus forcing the soil to turn over as the share cut through it.

It took a few grazed knuckles before I got it right.

When the days of chill depression came and Harry, sick in health and bank-balance, was struggling to keep faith with his beloved land it was time to put that training to the test.

Marking out a field had appeared to be easy until I tried. 'Set the furricker a good rod wide' — a furricker or headland being the space left for the horses to turn at either end of the field. I remembered that one rod, pole, or perch, equalled five of Harry's strides; seven of mine still left the horses with their noses through the hedge. My mark-line looked as if we had traced an outline of the inlets on some craggy island coast.

The test of a good ploughman 'opening up' a field is in getting the first furrow arrow-straight. The time-honoured way to do this is by tying paper to a thatching rod and standing it high in the hedge at the opposite end of the field. This acts as a guide, sightlined between the ears of the nearside horse all the way down the field.

If the plough is set correctly, with the horses pulling together and in step, if one can keep the reins taut and still grasp the handles to steer the plough over stony ground, the furrow will be straight. I knew all that but wished that I could explain the procedure to each uninterested horse. My permanently waved ploughed field became a local talking point all winter long.

I ploughed three fields that winter and the old men who congregated to put the world to rights in the blacksmith's forge agreed that if the first two had furrows as crooked as the hind leg of a knock-kneed mare, the third field was a 'fair old job'.

They advocated a continuous diet of 'beef pudden' to add the weight and stamina I lacked. At least the ploughing was finished before the back end of the year.

There is a country belief that to have the plough in the barn and the brist-board in the house on Christmas morning guarantees good crops at the following harvest. This is superstition based on fact. Frost makes ploughed earth friable and easier to work and the worst of the wintry weather comes in the New Year.

Harry mistrusted handling more horse power than he could stop with a sharp tug on the reins but reluctantly decided at last that he would have to go 'mechanised'.

The second-hand tractor salesman gave a demonstration drive round the stackyard, gave a brief discourse on the art of tractor driving, collected his money and left. The vibrating monster blew monoxide smoke rings from the upright exhaust as Harry climbed aboard.

With the full weight of his boot on the clutch, he ground the lever around the groaning gearbox until it obviously engaged, opened up the hand-throttle, lifted his boot and gazed steadfastly ahead. The tractor gathered speed — backward.

"Whoa there, whoa," he bellowed, tugging at the steering wheel as though reining in a headstrong horse. The tractor at full throttle reversed toward, then through, the splintering weatherboarded side of the barn. The revving engine spluttered, coughed and died.

The stalled silence was coloured by a repertoire of oaths as Harry invoked great balls of fire to descend upon his head if he should ever listen to a smooth-talking salesman or a horse-shy girl again.

He stumped off to the stable to regain his dignity and remove the splinters from his seat. He never attempted to drive again.

I couldn't leave the tractor snuggled up to the dribbling corn sacks, it looked all wrong.

THE SAGA OF FLORRIE FORD

The engine started reluctantly, and I found one of the three forward gears. I drove slowly through the barn doorway and, gathering speed and courage, did a lap of honour round the stack-yard, by which time I had been selected to be tractor driver to 'Florrie Ford'.

Life with Florrie Ford was never dull. She detested cold mornings and many a chivalrous male retired hurt, convinced that Florrie's starting handle had ruined his manhood and fractured his wrist for good measure. The answer to her sulking was to surprise her with some bicep-building swings, sprint round the mudguards of her iron-cleated wheels and waggle every control that moved.

With a following wind and a downhill run Florrie could notch up a good 10 m.p.h. in top gear.

With a 28lb. weight lashed under the seat to prevent me being tossed around like a bean in a bucket, ploughing, harrowing and cutting corn became easier thanks to Florrie Ford. We tackled land reclamation, tearing up twenty acres of sour pasture, the subsidy for which was four times the money Florrie had cost.

Any hesitation or misfiring responded to a thump on her fuel tank and I kept her going with cart-grease, wire and binder twine. This earned me the reputation of being mechanically minded.

Florrie chugged along for several years but one day she started to make internal rumblings going down a steep incline. The rumblings became a grinding clunk, Florrie stopped suddenly but the heavy load of feeding stuff hitched on behind did not.

I took a worm's eye view of a nettle bed and emerged to see Florrie on her side and definitely dead.

"Scrap iron. To think I wasted ten good pounds buying that old thing." Harry stared at the wrecked tractor in disgust and marched off to hitch his beloved horses to the plough.

Jim

A skein of plovers flying west were strung out like a black necklace across the sunset sky. From the saltings a curlew cried like a lost soul.

Out in the estuary a ship's siren wailed in melancholy unison and as the cold east wind rustled the rushes along the dykes, the familiar marsh became a desolate, God-forsaken, frightening place.

Following the rutted tyre marks of the lorry I hurried back toward the farm and slammed the marsh gate shut behind me.

Dad was walking dejectedly across the yard and as I caught up with him the floodgates of misery that had held fast all that dreadful afternoon suddenly gave way. Jim had been part of my life, all my life; now Jim was dead.

Both our mothers had been surprised to have us. Mum had given the iron rocking cot to the gipsies the year before I arrived, and on the day she brought me home from the hospital Dad found the old half-blind mare in the process of giving birth to Jim, a beautiful chestnut foal. So there we were, two unexpected offspring of ageing mothers.

Being an afterthought, I was often left to my own devices and long before either of us could see over, instead of through, the paddock gate Jim was my pet and playmate.

Even when he was old enough to work the fine young chestnut horse still had the ridiculous habit of sagging his forelegs, drooping his head over my shoulder and rubbing his neck along the side of my head.

He greeted the quietest of my three brothers in this way too but to strangers Jim would react like a devil horse, ears flat, tail swishing and back hooves flying.

Soon after I started school I was dared to call Jim from the playground and he jumped three hedges and the school fence to reach me, but the moment of glory was short-lived.

The bell that sent the children scuttling into lines brought the schoolmaster into the playground. I tried to pretend that the slobbering horse, his head resting on my shoulder, was a figment of the teacher's imagination.

The marks that his steel ruler made on my legs were proof that I failed. It was a very subdued child who led Jim back to the pasture by the forelock of his mane.

Dad realised that in Jim he had a possible prize winner for the local horse show. Harry Applethorn the wagoner decided that a horse pill would improve Jim's chances.

Administering a horse pill is a simple operation until you try to do it! Theoretically nothing could be easier than inserting a bullet-shaped pill into a hollow tube, placing one end of the tube at the back of the horse's throat, then blowing down the tube so that the pill shoots down the horse's neck.

Harry, a short man with legs so bandy he couldn't stop a pig in a passage, stood on a corn bin to administer the pill while Dad led the submissive horse into position to receive it.

Harry blew and Jim coughed simultaneously. There was a look of startled dismay on Harry's face; he gulped and after a burp that would keep a baby wind-free for months, Harry said that he had swallowed the pill.

JIM

He always reckoned afterwards that it cured his rheumatics.

It takes more preparation to get a horse ready for showing than it does to get a bride dressed up for her wedding. Jim was groomed for hours, his mane and tail braided with red, white and blue ribbons.

As he paraded around the show ring, high stepping his polished, dancing hooves, the chestnut horse was the most beautiful thing in my world.

When the judges held their final scrutiny Jim was among the final entries. Unable to contain my excitement, I ducked under the ropes at the edge of the ring and Jim was so pleased to see me that he sagged his head onto my shoulder.

I was hauled back by the seat of my cotton knickers, something snapped and I had to sit still after that! As if to demonstrate that he was fed up with being a fiery steed, Jim stood with his head down between his front hooves, looking more like a broken down clothes horse than a cup winner, which resulted in his gaining a 'highly commended' rosette instead of the coveted cup.

My brother used some binder twine to mend my drooping drawers and neither Jim nor myself were anybody's favourites on the way home.

On the day that Harry Applethorn passed out with pleurisy while driving to market, Jim had somehow known that he must turn the cart and bring him home.

We heard him coming up the slope at full trot until he stopped abruptly beside the garden fence, stamping and rattling his breastgirth impatiently.

No-one called Jim 'that fool horse' after that.

When war came, Jim and I, now in our twenties, were still together. During that summer, when our quiet country skies became a battlefield, we gathered in the harvest as the gallant few fought overhead.

One morning, when the vapour trails scrawled death across the clear blue canvas of the sky, Jim decided he was going back to the barn although we had scarcely started to load the wagon.

Nothing would calm him and we went back to the stock-yard with half a load.

An airbattle broke overhead and, as we watched, a bomber broke formation and hurtled, screaming, earthwards. As it reached the ground it disintegrated and the harvest field was littered with burning debris and exploding ammunition.

Young soldiers with old men's faces and eyes that mirrored the hell of Dunkirk helped us in the harvest season and, in our unchanging country ways, found healing respite before they faced the futility of war again.

Apart from that we relied on casual workers from the labour exchange and it was one of these who ended Jim's working days.

When men are afraid they arm themselves with weapons. This half-wit was scared of the playful, teasing horse and cut himself a long hazel switch.

Jim, who had never known cruelty, went berserk as the moronic fool lashed out at him with the hazel whip. Both horse and cart rolled over a steep bank. Jim never galloped again.

His weakened back made him walk like a tired old man and he spent the rest of his days grazing in the pasture on the edge of the marsh, coming in to his warm stall at night.

The unchanging pattern of seedtime and harvest went on despite the army lorries beneath the camouflage nets under the elm trees, the soldiers who were billeted in outhouses and an army workshop in the barn.

Frightfully efficient officers would gaze across the marsh, mutter about defence and security and more barbed wire and iron spikes would appear along the sea wall between the saltings and the marsh.

We often had to round up straying sheep and cattle because the soldiers had no time to worry about closing the marsh gates.

Complaining seemed futile — until one October afternoon.

JIM

A cold easterly gale made the elm trees creak and sigh so I went out to call Jim back to the warmth of the stable. The pasture was empty and the marsh gate swinging in the wind.

Impatient at the extra work and chilled by the biting wind, I hurried across the marsh but there was no sign of the old horse.

"Jim," I called, my voice doing battle with the whining, wailing wind. Knowing that he would come if he heard me, I ran along the dyke calling, calling. I found him in the sedge of the reed-filled ditch.

Black, stinking mud plastered his chestnut coat as he writhed in a devil's skein of barbed wire. Several coils of the dreadful stuff were scattered around.

Two small clips held each concertina-wound, tight-sprung, snaking coil and Jim must have sprung one with his hooves.

I took one look at the terrified struggling horse and ran, devil driven, to get help. With every breath tearing at the lining of my lungs I started the tractor, while Dad got ropes and pliers.

As we passed the soldiers we asked their help with wire cutters and sped on, every nut and bolt of the old tractor rattling in protest as it was driven full throttle over the bumpy marsh.

The next half-hour 'was an unending nightmare as we struggled with the wire and pulled Jim from the morass and all the time his eyes followed me, imploring help.

We stood covered with filthy slime, hands and clothes torn, our own blood mingling with Jim's, and a sergeant who had left Europe by way of Dunkirk went into the reeds and was violently sick.

Dad went off to do the only thing we could to help the old horse now while I knelt beside the panting animal, stroking his torn neck and talking to him until gradually he quietened.

He tried to lift his head and instinctively I knew what he

wanted me to do. It seemed an eternity before I heard the slaughterer's lorry coming across the marsh but, cramped, cold and stunned, I still managed to hold Jim's head on my shoulder.

As the lorry came close Jim moved his head and tried to rub his neck against me as he had always done, but suddenly it became too heavy to hold.

I let his head slip gently to the ground.

The horse slaughterer didn't need to use the humane killer he was carrying.

The soldiers cleared up the wire and the lorry went off with its pathetic cargo.

"It's just a casualty of war," said the sergeant. I felt a desperate need to be alone and volunteered to walk back and close the gates.

A skein of plovers were strung out like a black necklace across the sunset sky. From the saltings a curlew cried like a lost, tormented soul and from the estuary a ship's siren called in dismal unison. The once-loved marsh became an eerie, hateful place.

Following the rutted tyre marks of the lorry I ran towards the farm and slammed the marsh gate shut behind me.

The hut

The village Cultural and Recreational Memorial Hall sounds somewhat impressive considering that it was an ex-Army workshop, bought cheap on site at the end of World War 1.

We called it The Hut and, despite constant patching and shoring-up, it was reaching the limit of durability.

The moment of truth came during the Harvest Home Supper, when a section of the plaster-board ceiling parted company with the rafters.

Having graciously received the traditional bouquet, our distinguished guest of honour collected ceiling-white and dust in her freshly set blue rinse as the remnants of a starling's nest made splash-down in her soup.

Tom Grommet slipped home to collect a hammer and nails while we all moved along a place, just like the Mad Hatter's tea party.

Everyone tried to laugh off the episode as jolly rollicking fun, but it was plain that the evening had lost its magic for our guest. She discarded the notes of her after-dinner speech, tersely suggested that we start a rebuilding fund and left before Will could begin his annual rendition of *'Buttercup Joe'*.

There is a mountain of money between recognising the need for a new village hall and being able to build one. Like seed sown on stony ground, the crop of cash or fund-raising schemes was pretty sparse.

Earlier generations had managed to transform an Army hut into a village hall and, seeking inspiration from their example, we looked back through The Hut committee books.

The grand inaugural happening was a church social and the minutes of the very first meeting record the vicar's disapproval of the purchase of French chalk for making dancing possible on the unpolished surface of the floor.

Still stored in the ladies' cloakroom, behind a box marked Coronation Bunting 1937, is a framed notice forbidding any gentleman to swing or lift his dancing partner off the floor, or dance in so close proximity as to be unseemly.

For a 'Cultural' hall, edifying activities appear to have been spread thinly down the years. A neighbouring curate and his wife gave occasional piano and cello recitals, labouring valiantly with an out of tune piano and a cello that was never quite on key.

It takes a powerful imagination to envisage farm-hands flocking from the fields to sing along in 'An Evening Of Toccatas And Fugues.' Give or take a few, the duo seems to have had a faithful following of eight.

Their performance of *Air On A G String* had more response but I am given to understand that, thanks to the New American movies, the audience was mostly adolescent youth under some delusion as to what a G string really meant.

Fan's Failings: A Morality Play must have been a mind-bending cultural experience. One uncensorable scene called for the villain to catch Fan in the kitchen, compromised by the absence of her blouse. Rather than risk inflaming the male populace the modest Fan demanded that she be allowed to wear her camisole above instead of underneath her petticoat and vest.

This was pretty racy stuff according to local standards but Fan displayed her naked forearms in the cause of culture and it is not on record that any of the audience went berserk.

Against the vicar's dissenting vote, The Hut became a gambling hell of cribbage drives and whist on every second and fourth Wednesday of the month.

The hand-printed posters advertising any village festivity always carried the proviso, 'If wet, in The Hut' and the records show that despite the belief that the sun shines on the righteous the vicarage fete seemed singularly unfortunate in its choice of weather through the years.

I am left-handed, with a tendency to take off in the opposite direction when asked to turn to the left or right, a failing later responsible for getting a driving test examiner disorientated and lost on his own testing route.

At the fete in question I was detailed for the school maypole dancing team. Dressed all in white, with paper flowers in my hair and clutching my coloured streamer as if it were the bearing rein of a wayward horse, I clumped through *Gathering Peascods,* remembering my strict instructions to 'follow the girl in front'. Halfway through *Ruffti-Tuffti,* chaos! I lost track of my pathfinder and found that I was travelling in the opposite direction to all the rest.

Pressing on regardless, my maypole ribbon became a tripwire, leaving the other dancers lying around in heaps with the ribbons just a multi-coloured knot.

It took a king-sized pair of scissors to sort out the muddle and believe me, one has never plumbed the depths of humiliation until one has had one's maypole streamer publicly pruned.

There were village concerts every year, but none was more ambitious than the 'Welcome Home' effort at the end of the last war. The entire village seemed to be involved. No opportunity for rehearsal was lost.

The blacksmith's wife became the Spirit of Freedom and

Light and her part in the grand finale should have been sheer show-stopping spectacle.

She stood on a cider barrel centre stage, supporting her banner of freedom and brandishing her flame of light. Actual flames being somewhat risky in a wooden building with a pitched felt roof, the torch effect was achieved by disguising a battery-lit cycle lamp in silver paper hung around with the anti-radar metal foil strips that wartime aircraft used to drop.

Unfortunately the initial impact of this scene was lost.

Where curtain up should have revealed a darkened stage lit only by the Flame of Light illuminating the Banner of Freedom, a glow-worm of light from a flat battery shone on to the face of the blacksmith's wife as she appealed to any cycle-riding, public spirited member of the audience to let her borrow a front lamp.

Mis-cued, unheralded and unlit, the flag-bearing cast representing 'Our Gallant Allies' stumbled across the stage.

There were minor skirmishes and chaos reigned supreme. It was a howling success and there has been nothing to match it ever since.

Nowadays fund-raising village concerts are just not on.

Television-satiated as we are, no-one turns out on a wet wintry night to hear *On The Road To Mandalay* sung in a voice that developed a flat tyre just north of Chittagong.

Our Tramps Supper seemed a social success and looked to be a financial winner until, comparing notes while washing up, we realised that the gentleman so scruffily disguised was no-one's invited guest but the genuine article, contributing only his 'livestock' in exchange for a slap-up meal and the secretary's purse.

Simple, memorable occasions have made The Hut part of the fabric of our lives. Wedding receptions, harvest suppers, parties, all have been entered in the old ledger that opens with the account of the acquisition of one ex-Army hut and a plot of adjoining waste land.

The market value of this waste land has now made it

possible to plan the new village hall, a real and much needed asset to the community. No-one bothered about acoustics or amenities in The Hut, yet past laughter and happiness must have soaked into every wood-worm-riddled board. To watch it being dismantled will be like tearing up a favourite comfortable coat.

Sam Lamb

Regularly during the winter a flock of mallard flew across the valley to their distant feeding grounds out on the mud-flats of the estuary.

On the dreary days when mist has clung clammy and damp as a wet sheep's fleece we still heard a stirring of wings and conversational quacking as the mallard passed overhead at daybreak and each afternoon.

One day their routine was altered. As they passed, the leading drake broke formation, wheeled and glided down to settle on Church Field pond. He spread his wings, duck-dancing across the surface to display the irridescence of his plumage. His companions, confused and calling, circled in disorder, separated, then flew on.

One drab female turned back, losing height, then flew down beside him, fluttering her wings in courtship as she joined her new-found partner in a cacophonous duck duet.

Moorhens foraging in the rough grass of Church Field went scurrying back towards the pond, ludicrous comedians in green and yellow tights and flippered feet, their heads all jerking forward with each exaggerated comic step.

There was a lot of disyllabic croaking and quarrelling before the waterfowl conceded that the mallard had established squatters' rights on Church Field pond and they must exist together in a state of cautious neutrality.

It happens every year.

Even the gregarious rooks sensed that there was an indefinable difference in the day. Since early morning the colony had been noisily arguing in the elm boughs or disengaging from aerial combat to fly down and strut menacingly towards another rival, ignored completely by the placid grazing sheep.

A few amiable birds were already inspecting last year's nests, refurbishing with neighbours' twigs, indignantly protesting if another pair attempted to raid their own.

Dutch elm disease had reduced the trees in the rookery and the siting of new nests would give some indication as to the weather ahead, according to the old country lore, 'Rooks build high: calm, fair and dry; rooks build low: cold, wet and blow.'

There was a new warmth on the wind, the sun was out and the land stirred from cold winter's sleep. Birds sought their mates and from this day shepherds knew that they must watch their ewes, no matter when lambing was due to start.

My prosaic Mum had a name for this one day. She called it 'Bedspread Washday', symbolising her salute to spring.

This was no ordinary laundering Monday, formidable as they were with the basic preparation for washday being to first cut up a tree, light the copper fire and pump water from the well.

There was a copper on each side of the open fireplace in the farmhouse scullery.

In earlier times the larger copper had been used for beer brewing and scalding fresh-killed pork. The smaller had the mundane purpose of providing bath water and coping with

the weekly wash. On Mum's Bedspread Washday both coppers were stoked and filled.

Bedspread Washday was a devil's sabbath with every currant bush sprouting cushion covers and fringed plush tablecloths. Between the line-posts honeycombed counterpanes and patchwork quilts billowed in the breeze and on impromptu clothes lines between two plum trees mattress tickings and unwieldy chair covers flapped water on the unwary walking up the garden path.

Indoors, the witches' cauldron coppers produced a soap and soda fog, from which emerged my Bedspread Washday Mum. Not her usual easy-going self, but a Mum all shiny faced with the bun of her hair askew and each wisp lank with dew-droplets of steam.

A 'chop-more-firewood', 'turn-the-mangle', 'pump-more-water' Mum, quick to anger, hard to please.

Bedspread Washday dinner, 'bubble and squeak', impregnated with the taste of primrose soap. No pud. No tablecloth. A meal served on the still damp whitewood kitchen table, copper-water scrubbed. One learned to eat up and go.

Dad was always sure to need a hand with thatching the hurdle gates to make lambing-pens, or one could volunteer to go around the sheep and check that no in-lamb ewes had rolled over on to their backs, something that happens to pregnant ewes. Their struggling to regain their feet can exhaust them and cause death.

It was on such a Bedspread Washday that I found Sam.

A sheep will usually clean its new-born lamb until it bleats and struggles to its feet and if the lamb does not respond the mother's distress is very real. When I found Sam his mother was grazing disinterestedly some way away.

At first I thought that I had found a premature still-born lamb but as I picked up the minute cold body I felt a butterfly fluttering heartbeat. Holding him in one hand and pressing his ribcage with the other started respiration.

Sam gave a feeble bleat.

Cade, or hand-reared lambs, were nothing new, as there were one or two weaklings or orphans every year, but Sam was the smallest lamb I had ever seen. I popped him into my woollen mitten, tucked him down inside my coat and hurried home.

The kitchen fireplace was barricaded by two huge old-fashioned clothes-horses draped with airing bedcovers.

Wrapped in an old flannel nightie in a shoe box on the hooked rag hearthrug, Sam might well have been in a purpose-built incubator.

By evening he had acquired a taste for milk laced with brandy but the problem now was how to keep him warm all night. There can't be many lambs that are carried upstairs wrapped in a flannel nightie, wearing a tea-towel nappy and improvised sponge-bag waterproof pants. I kept him warm that night. By morning Sam was trying to balance himself on weak and wobbly legs.

From that point life revolved around Sam's frequent feeding times. He followed me everywhere and tried to converse in grunts and bleats. Being adopted by a lamb small enough to wriggle through a sheep-proof fence means waiting at the village bus stop, all dressed up to go to town with the black-smith's son and seeing Sam trit-trotting down the lane, piti-fully bleating 'Maa'.

The bus conductor was perplexed. Fare scales for dogs he understood, but passenger lambs were not catered for on the company schedule. Consulting the driver, he decided that Sam would travel free. If the bus inspector came aboard I might try to disguise Sam as a pair of sheep-skin gloves.

The bus crews had changed shift for the return journey and the new conductor had a disagreeable face. Sam travelled home in a twopenny carrier bag from the fish and chip shop, while a friendly fellow passenger sat with 'Two of cod and six of chips' newspaper-wrapped on her lap.

Sam never grew large enough to contemplate his being sent to market and we would never let him run the risk of being eaten with mint sauce, but he had his uses. Turned out among a flock of sheep, he would come running when I called.

The others would always follow him and, like the eastern shepherds, we could lead our sheep instead of driving them along, thanks to Sam Lamb.

At the sign of the star

Mid-December brought a howling north-east gale that roared across the valley, flinging the full force of its fury against the farm.

For days it raged, then swung round to become a whining easterly wind that penetrated every crevice of the house and sent one two-coat-clad to work about the farm.

At night the new moon rose blood red and tilted on its back, a sure sign that we should shovel snow before it waned.

By now the cattle had been brought down off the hills to shelter in the warmth of the enclosed yard. The Hereford bullocks, like a group of disapproving aunts glaring at a precocious child, disdainfully twitched steaming nostrils as the half-grown collie pup chased imaginary rats from the straw I scattered in the yard. Soon they were hock deep and the pup floundered in litter that was deep enough to last two days.

Tomorrow would be Christmas Day, yet in the isolation of the farm, with no sound but the cattle chewing the cud and a flight of starlings chattering their way to roost in the high holly hedge, it seemed like any other working day. I thought of town-bred girls and momentarily envied them their brightly-decorated, bustling shops, their office parties and the centrally heated warmth. They never went to work wrapped like lumbering Eskimos, yet I would never really want to leave the farm and have my parents struggle on alone.

A sound to conjure up high summer cut across my thoughts above the starlings' din and the flapping of the galvanised sheet that had come adrift from the wind-wrecked hen house.

I heard the sound again. The pup heard it too and raced along the farm track to the lane but soon returned, his tail between his legs. Snapping at his heels was a narrow-gutted whippet, thin enough to show each rib beneath his sandy skin.

A combination of ungreased axles, roughshod hooves, clanking buckets and drag chains makes a gipsy caravan sound unmistakeable in some undefinable way. A sound that goes with warm haymaking days and harvest time, for in my world gipsies appeared in early summer and vanished when harvest ended.

To see one in the lane on Christmas Eve was very odd indeed.

It turned into our gate, a dilapidated canvas-hooded cart pulled by a shaggy, thickset cob. A tall young gipsy wearing a week's growth of beard and a baggy old army greatcoat tied round with binder twine led the tired horse. I went to meet him.

"The guv'nor about?" he asked. Dad, seeing our visitor, had hurried back from the kale field.

"You can't stop here!" he said, before the gipsy even asked.

The young man wanted to pull his wagon to the leeward side of the holly hedge, promising that he would move on at dawn, but Dad was adamant.

"I don't doubt that you will be gone, along with all the fowls!"

The Gipsy flushed. "I'm no Dideki, moosh! Joe Kemp gives you his word! I saw old Uncle Manny's sign beside your gate and thought you would let me unhitch here tonight. Old Manny once sold you a horse."

Dad remembered the patriarchal old Romany, whose family group had worked the fields some seven years before and asked if he were still alive. The gipsy smiled.

"Oh, Dordi. I'm heading for his winter camp before the weather breaks. He's got a warm new wagon waiting for me there. Go on 'chavi', let me stay tonight, the old girl's back is hurting her something cruel and the nag is walking on its knees."

Mum came into the yard and Joe explained that he had been picking sprouts to earn enough money to buy the new wagon, but his woman wasn't well so he had headed back east to rejoin his tribe.

Joe's 'old girl' had remained inside the cart but now the flap was pulled aside and we saw the anxious face of a girl no older than myself. Mum looked at her then whispered to Dad who shrugged his shoulders in resignation. Tiny Mum was taking charge! She spoke gently to the girl, climbed the three-rung ladder into the cart, then emerged again.

"The poor thing's miserably cold and in considerable pain."

Addressing Joe from the height of his third rib she added,

"Young man, you will have to travel fast to get to winter camp before the baby arrives!"

Because the frozen canvas cover was as draughtproof as a moth-eaten sack, Dad allowed Joe to pull the van into the open-fronted cart shed, its tin stovepipe chimney protruding at the back. We went back to finishing our tasks, keeping a watchful eye on the 'Gippos' as we worked.

The smell of the soup Mum carried across the yard in a big blue jug made me feel glad to get in for my tea in the cosy kitchen and our visitors in the cart shed receded from our thoughts as Christmas Eve preparations progressed.

We were reminded of their presence by a hammering on the

100

door.

Mum and Dad rushed out thinking that the cart shed was going up in smoke, but an agitated Joe said,

"My old girl is taken bad. You've got a kind face lady. For God's sake come and help."

The girl crouched beside a biscuit-tin sized stove, her eyes having the same terrified expression as a wild animal in a trap. Mum got her to the bunk-like bed, its linen remarkably clean and white.

We had no phone, the district nurse was miles away and it was obvious that the baby was impatient to be born. Mum suggested taking the girl into the house, but both husband and wife were determined that their true-bred Romany son was not to be born under a 'gorgio's' roof. However they agreed that no newborn babe could survive in ten degrees of frost and compromised by accepting the use of the lambing shed, an outhouse with an open fireplace that had saved the lives of countless new-born orphan lambs, and Joe went off to light the fire.

The baby settled the question by arriving with an almighty yell which brought Joe running back across the yard.

"Dordi, moosh! I've got a son. I'll call him Manny, since old Manny's sign guided me here."

Midnight saw us cutting up Mum's flannel petticoats to clothe the newborn child and mother and babe were settled for the night. We saw a shooting star as we crossed the yard to go indoors; a sign, Mum said, of a newborn babe.

Joe bought the ruined hen house and our Christmas Day was punctuated by the sound of hammering in the cart shed. By Boxing Night the cart had taken on a most peculiar shape, for Joe had completely covered the canvas hood with tin, making it weatherproof and relatively free from draughts.

The ice was melting in the cattle troughs next day and high banked snowclouds were building in the sky when Joe hitched up the horse and backed the cart up to the lambing shed door. With his wife wrapped up in one of Mum's goose feather quilts and the baby snug in his orange box crib, Joe was ready to move off.

"We're 'Kushti', now, Guv, thank you kindly." He took Dad's right hand and clapped it to his own, a Romany gesture of good faith. Turning his head he called; "You right there, Mary girl?" and the reply was lost in the noise of the rattling cart.

Dad and I followed them along the farm track to the gate.

"I wonder what old Emmanuel Kemp will think of his namesake," Dad reflected, but something strange had clicked in my mind.

"Dad, Joe called his wife Mary, the baby's name is Emmanuel and he was born among the cattle at Christmas."

Dad saw my line of thought. "Look love, it's coincidence. Joseph Kemp is a Romany, his wife an ordinary girl and they only stopped here because of a gipsy mark somewhere beside our gate."

The thoughts of this kind of bush telegraph intrigued me and as the wagon rolled down the lane and out of sight I searched round for the sign.

Some minutes later, on the smooth bark of the beech tree by the gate, I found the symbol Old Manny cut some seven years before. It was carved in the shape of a Star of Bethlehem.

The luck
of the bees

Busy as a scuttling field mouse, Madge was gathering dandelions along the old wood road.

"Late they are this year," she said, her scrabbling fingers furiously decapitating flower heads.

"Dandelions should be fit to pick for making wine on St. George's Day."

Eyes that do not really notice what they see could dismiss as weeds the plants that Madge turns into wines, lotions and healing balms. She seems to know the name and location of every wild flower growing along the isolated paths she wandered as a child. Madge's father had been a drover.

These men would, single handed, undertake to drive flocks of sheep or herds of cattle over long distances between the upland pastures or farms and the cattle fairs, stock sales, and markets that were held throughout the year.

Motherless, Madge had accompanied her father along most of the old droving tracks that criss-cross the southern part of the country, walking all the way.

In a childhood not over-blessed with soft living, Madge's first memories are of being buffeted by scampering sheep the same height as herself and sleeping under a tarpaulin shelter, snuggled up against a tick-scratching collie dog in an effort to keep warm.

With the onset of winter Madge would be boarded out while her father lodged at a men's hostel near the city market, undertaking short journey work.

Sometimes pity would stir a kind-hearted country woman to offer shelter to the waif Madge must have been, but all too frequently it was a strictly commercial transaction.

Ask Madge her age and all that she can verify is that she is as old as her tongue and a little older than her teeth. She thinks that she must have been about nine during the winter that she ran away.

"Dad and I had walked a flock of sheep to Stow Fair in Gloucestershire that autumn," Madge recalls.

But their stay in the town was only short, for her father had the prospect of taking an enormous flock seventy miles across country and wanted to get started before some other drover undercut his price.

"It began to rain in torrents as we left the village of Stow and somehow I just knew that the coming winter would be bad." It was.

The journey over the Cotswolds, bleak with gale-driven rain, was a nightmare. Sheep, lame with footrot, held up their progress and the father, frantic to reach their destination, knew he would never get there hampered by an exhausted child.

Had circumstances been better, Madge is convinced that he would never have left her with the 'minder' as he did.

As soon as the money for her keep and winter clothes had changed hands and her father had gone on his way there was no pretence that she would be treated as one of the family, 'the family' being a hard-faced woman and two loutish sons.

Their treatment of her was so bad that Madge knew that to survive she must try to find her father.

These then were the circumstances that half a century ago sent Madge, sick, sore and starving, past the cottage on the edge of Penny-pot Wood.

A rat trap seems a singularly unlikely instrument of destiny, but the occupants of Penny-pot Cottage, troubled by rats in the hen house, had set one beneath some brushwood by the hedge.

Madge, passing, saw the hard cheese bait and in trying to spring the trap caught her foot in the steel teeth.

Gentle hands released her and carried her into Penny-pot Cottage, a new life and a new home.

Madge still recalls the heaven of lying on a worn leather sofa with both feet wrapped in warm poulticed linen, drinking warm milk and eating crusty bread thick with butter and honey.

By the next morning when she woke it was settled that she should stay with Aunty Beech, as she was told to call her new-found guardian, until her father came for her.

But first they would have to tell the bees.

Young as she was, Madge had encountered madness on her travels. Was this bee nonsense the worm in the apple of her new paradise? Aunty Beech led her around to the back of the house and addressed the roof.

"This is Madge. With your approval she has come to stay."

Madge was shown the room where she would stay, providing that she kept herself scrupulously clean and did nothing to offend the bees. It had a sloping ceiling, marred near the dormer window by a moist golden brown stain which oozed a sticky substance that occasionally dripped down into a large white jug.

There had been a swarm of bees in the cottage roof for time out of mind and in all probability the penny pots of honey sold at the cottage door gave name to the house, the woodland and the lane.

They certainly provided Aunty Beech with the basis of her livelihood and like a magnet drew generations of children to spend their precious halfpennies and farthings at the cottage in Penny-pot Lane.

By the time I was old enough to realise that Penny-pot ginger-beer and home-made sweets were an economical proposition Madge was grown up and Miss Beech an old lady who spent most of her days watching the bees at work.

In May and June she kept a bunch of keys handy in case the bees should swarm.

Claiming the ancient law of right of way to pursue her swarming bees, she once entered the Manor House.

She marched straight through the front entrance and out of the back door, clashing the keys on the frying pan as she ran. When they settled she collected them and took them home in her straw hat.

It was worth the long walk to Penny-pot Cottage to buy nutty toffee and ginger beer made in stone bottles with corks that came out with a champagne pop, half-penny a foaming glass. My mind's tongue tastes it now.

Miss Beech maintained that bees could foretell bad weather and bad news. They were in a state of turmoil on the day she died but, remembering instructions, Madge told them of her passing and begged them to stay under her protection and not take their luck away.

Health regulations forbid the continuation of the sweet-shop in Penny-pot Cottage parlour but Madge still sells honey and uses her knowledge of herbs and the places where they grow.

You might see her driving her old car to the herbalist store in the town, or out along some lonely country drove.

Hillside tracks where no bracken grows, overgrown lanes, pilgrims paths, Roman roads, routes marked only by dotted lines on maps: the old drover's routes still exist, the places where a drover's half-starved daughter and a tick-infested collie once walked.

A dog
called Moses

Yard dogs were frequently unhappy, neglected creatures.
More than a few outlying farms had a wretched collie
tethered to a draughty barrel for a kennel, dragging out its
existence on a length of rusting chain.

Kept to deter prowling foxes or warn off unwelcome strangers, they deteriorated into whimpering apathetic curs or
became ferocious hysterical manhaters. If one broke free it
invariably ran berserk, attacking cattle, sheep and fowls and
had to be destroyed.

Working dogs fared somewhat better. Only a minority of
shepherds believed that a hungry dog, trained to fear its master, would round up sheep more efficiently than a well-fed pet.
Most shepherds took pride in the breeding, physical condition
and prowess of their dogs, yet one of the greatest canine
characters I ever encountered would have been laughed out
of the arena at any sheepdog trials.

His name was Moses. Hugh found him in the rushes by the
road up on High Common, a windswept wilderness of wheel-

ing lapwings, stunted gorse and Hugh's summer-grazing sheep. A small-built man of interminable energy, Hugh tried to make a living from hill farming the upland pastures of High Common and his twenty-acre hired holding down below the hill.

His wife, having to make every copper count, begrudged the cost of feeding a pup too amiable in disposition for a yard-dog and certainly not bred to work with sheep.

There was much speculation about the background of a pup which had inherited the characteristic drooping ears and large paws of a spaniel, the bone formation and facial expression of a labrador, a rag-bag mixture of grey, black and brown curled coat and no tail to wag at all.

But Moses stayed, growing rapidly and developing an almost telepathic understanding of his master. Soon after he arrived Mrs. Hugh caught Moses trying out his bark for size, then watching the reactions of her flustered hens.

She made a ruff of quill feathers, a country cure for chicken chasers, threatening to tie it around his neck and leave it there until it dropped off.

Moses took the hint and ignored the chickens. Within months Moses needed no more instructions than a conversational "Let's get those darn fool ewes over here then" to send him off to round up the flock. He had become a lolloping knock-about clown of a dog, liable to catch his long flapping ears under his front paws and turn somersaults when the ground was rough.

Hugh drove a battered hard-topped jeep purchased, so rumour had it, in a pub at closing time in 1945. The States-bound American sergeant swore that it was definitely war surplus stock since he would not be needing it again but Hugh wasted no time in covering its camouflaged bodywork in the same red oxide that he was using to paint a galvanised tin roof.

Crouched low over the steering wheel with Moses at his side Hugh in his old jeep became part of the local scene and more than one person had reason to remember his tendency to cut the engine and coast down hills.

November mist shrouded the hillside as a quaking sales-man staggered into the village pub, convinced that he had encountered the occult. He had stopped to clean his wind-screen up on High Common and swore that a ghostly army truck driven by a leering dog-faced devil with huge hairy hands had materialised out of the mist, glided noiselessly past and disappeared.

No-one mentioned Hugh's left hand drive jeep or Moses's habit of sitting with his front paws on the dash. The salesman paid for several rounds before his courage returned and he drove away.

Soon after, Hugh and Moses were involved in a much earth-ier incident. Hugh was not averse to acquiring any sort of fertiliser to improve the productivity of his smallholding and he knew where there was some pig-manure that could almost be termed a liquid asset. Loading an empty 100 gallon tank into the jeep, he drove over to the other side of the common as soon as it was dark.

While Hugh was busy with bucket and shovel a police patrol, pursuing a notorious law-breaker reported to have been sighted in the vicinity, set up a checkpoint on the bridge at the bottom of the hill.

They heard a vehicle cut its engine and come coasting down the lane.

With torches flashing they signalled it to stop. Hugh slammed on the brakes but the lurching sudden halt set up a backwash of pig manure, engulfing Hugh and Moses and settl-ing inches deep over the floor. The policeman on the offside was flattened by a flying muck-covered dog but Hugh, sub-merged in misery, sat trying to explain. One could smell as well as see Hugh's jeep approaching after that.

In the dusk of an early spring evening Hugh, with Moses at his heels, took a last look around the lambing ewes on the hill. The flock were settling peacefully but Moses, restless, stood trembling and sniffing at the wind, his hackles raised and thunder rumbling in his throat.

Hugh had never seen him so disturbed and wondered what was wrong; then in the dusk he discerned a shape more wolf than dog sidling down towards, the flock like some loping beast of prey.

The first disturbed ewe stood nervously stamping and calling to her lamb. The maurauding yelping dog broke cover, throwing the lamb high in the air and ripping through the fleece of its mother.

Hugh was not carrying his gun and knew that Moses was no match for the killer dog. He ordered him to stay. For the first time in years Moses disobeyed.

Hugh ran toward the carnage of torn sheep and the furious flailing mass of flying bloodflecked fur that was the fighting dogs.

He eventually drove off the killer, still trailing its broken chain. Moses lay quite still.

With daylight there would be more dead ewes and stillborn lambs. Tomorrow Hugh would find out whose yard-dog was missing and alert his neighbours to hunt for the killer.

Meanwhile it was getting dark and he had a hole to dig.

It's just not cricket

Those misguided enough to have been born over at Lockley Green would have you believe that one could come to our village as a babe in arms, remain here all one's life and still be an old foreigner when one was planted six foot deep. It's what is called living in a close-knit community.

Time was when any local girl caught glancing sideways at a lad from Lockley way ran the risk of feeling the flat side of her father's hand. The rivalry between the two communities has mellowed somewhat since the days when duckpond dunking was an inter-village sport and now we meet for a 'friendly' match at the start of every cricket season.

But make no mistake, there is no idealistic nonsense that it is the game that matters and not the result when our village team plays Lockley Green. It is the score that counts and gamesmanship is such a practised art that one could believe the Ashes were at stake.

As pitches go, Lockley club have every right to feel superior. Their pitch, encircled by majestic horse-chestnut trees, is

111

in the home farm paddock of 'The Park'. Our pitch was quaint rather than picturesque when it was on the village green.

Hardly spacious, cramped perhaps, a straight drive from the snowplough end invariably meant that some unfortunate fielder sent to retrieve the ball from Granny Gammon's garden ran the gauntlet of being chased by an evil tempered old gander and his gaggle of hissing geese.

Now that 'granny's place' has gone and bungalows with huge picture windows skirt the green, tiddly-winks would be a safer game to play. Hugh from High Common Farm volunteered the use of one of his pastures as a pitch and if our team has a secret weapon, psychologically speaking, Banky Meadow is it.

It tends to demoralise visiting teams to find that our cricket pitch is sited halfway up a hill. It has been known for new fixtures, disorientated from driving around the lanes endeavouring to find the field, to draw up at the gate, stare at our sloping pitch in disbelief, then depart before Albert our club hon. sec. can get down to welcome them and undo the wire that ties up the gate.

That wire is a necessity, for the club shares Banky Meadow's fifteen acres with three redundant rams and thirteen inquisitive Hereford heifers. At practices and home matches a group of small boys are bribed to keep them at the far end of the field, but they seem to take an intense interest in the game and frequently outnumber spectators two to one.

Their presence tends to unnerve the fielding opposition, not used to having to watch out where they put their feet.

It makes no difference if the pitch is 'holding moisture' or not. If we win the toss our team bats first, the theory being that the opposition will be so exhausted with all the running up and down hill that their protesting calf muscles will inhibit their ability to score.

There is another advantage in batting early on. By tea-time the sun is behind the bowler's arm from the cattle-shed end and many a Lockley wicket has been lost on this account.

Don't imagine that we have no facilities. We have. Our pavilion is rain-proof if nothing else. It may not be so architecturally pleasing as Lockley's. That was built to commemorate the twenty-first birthday of an Edwardian squire's son, known to earlier generations as 'The Right Horrible Fred'.

Ours was donated by a local supporter who went over from open range chicken farming and wanted his largest henhouse shifted to make space for his battery sheds. It may not have a clock tower as Lockley pavilion does, but you would be surprised what useful lockers nest boxes can make.

Albert Parsley has worked wonders converting the place. When farm wagons were still being made down at old Humph's yard, Albert was the chap who painted them and did the distinctive decoration with squiggly fine lines. Now he potters, painting everything and anything he can.

Albert was never very popular over Lockley Way, having got a girl from Lockley Bottoms to the altar steps before his commonsense and local pride made him marry a village girl instead. It was a local victory when 'young Albert', as he was then, was commissioned by the squire to repaint the face of Lockley pavilion clock.

Very smart it looked too, but for several undetected years it marked the passage of time with five dividing lines between each roman numeral. No-one noticed.

Albert kept his practical joke against Lockley to himself until, goaded by successive defeats at bowls, cricket and the annual tug-of-war, he taunted the jeering Lockley-ites as being the only village where they worked for seventy-two minutes to the hour by the clock and never knew they were doing so.

Now Albert amuses himself by painting the cricket club score-board in Old English script. He has made a special set of number plates to hang on it when we play Lockley Green. Try reading a cricket score in Roman numerals. Psychological warfare at its worst.

IT'S JUST NOT CRICKET

As batsmen, the Chappel family from the dairy have always provided the backbone of our team. With organisation, the problem of their having to nip home at milking time is overcome. Substitutes cover the fielding side and if perchance they stay in while their comrades' wickets all fall, the stalwart supporter ladies who spend hours spreading marge and slicing cucumber for sandwiches turn off the oil stove under the tea urn.

Having done so they then apologise for the delay in serving tea and listen for Hugh's old jeep returning, holding up proceedings long enough to give the band of volunteers a chance to help the Chappels with their chores between batting and fielding.

No-one will admit it, but to my mind this year's brand of gamesmanship has reached the ultimate where our local derby is concerned.

The first match with Lockley is an away game. Perce the postman, giving a daily report on the state of their pitch, said that he had never seen it looking better.

An inbred hang-up from the forelock clutching days when village kids knew better than to beat 'The Right Horrible Fred' at the races that were held on Lockley cricket pitch makes us tread carefully on its turf, as if the wicket were hallowed ground.

But it was something less than perfect for this year's match and looked as if it had broken out in a brown soil rash.

"Dear me," said a member of our team who shall be nameless.

"I thought that Banky Meadow was the only place round here to be plagued with moles. Set mole traps up there this year and you can catch 'em two at a time. Do a lot of damage overnight, moles can!"

Whatever else it is, it's hardly cricket.

An arch of
iron flowers

Walk along any village street and you will notice that most
old cottages still have a horse-shoe nailed, points uppermost,
to the lintel of the door. If one house appears to defy
superstition by having a reversed horse-shoe above the thres-
hold the chances are that this is where the blacksmith lived.

Until recently, customs and beliefs dating from pre-
Christian times still prevailed among those whose livelihood
depended on the land. Being at the mercy of nature and the
soil was a very chancy business.

By placating whatever powers ruled the seasons they hoped
to escape ill-fortune on the land and in the home.

Iron was believed to ward off evil influences. An iron poker
placed upright against the bars of a sulking fire would drive
the devil from the hearth.

A horse-shoe placed above the entrance to a dwelling was
double insurance. It would deter malevolent spirits from enter-
ing and, providing that the points were kept uppermost, the
good fortune already in the house would not escape.

AN ARCH OF IRON FLOWERS

The blacksmith, by the very nature of his trade, was immune from evil influences and witchcraft; an upturned horse-shoe was the symbol of his trade.

A master-farrier had the right to mount three reversed horse-shoes in pyramid formation above the entrance to his smithy and his home. The smithy was the news centre for farming and local gossip.

The smith was a key craftsman, respected and relied on by a community which depended on his skill in using iron for their plough-shares, coulters and harrows and for keeping their horses shod.

The technique of horse-shoeing has remained unaltered for centuries, as has the apprenticeship and training for the black-smith's and farrier's trades.

Bert, our village blacksmith, came from a long line of craftsmen, but it was not customary for a smith to train his own son. Being small in stature when he left school, Bert spent three years as beer-boy, pumping the huge pear-shaped bellows of the forge fire for most part of the time. He was seventeen when his articled apprenticeship began.

The unpunctuated indenture papers read like some medieval document whereby he signed that he would 'faithfully guard his master's secrets, neither waste, lend or sell his master's goods'. He would not 'absent himself from his master's service by day or night, but in all things act as a faithful apprentice toward his said master and all of his'.

In return his master promised to teach and instruct, 'finding sufficient meat, drink, lodgings and all other necessities'.

By his twentieth birthday Bert was earning ten shillings a week and ending the first part of his apprenticeship.

The second part would not start until he had passed a traditional test of strength.

He would still be regarded as 'the boy' until he could put his forearms under the anvil and lift it clear of the smithy floor. It made sense; a blacksmith needs strength as well as skill. A sway-backed shire horse, weighing over a ton and reluctant to be shod, has an uncomfortable tendency to lean on the farrier when its hoof is lifted off the ground.

Lifting the anvil was a ritual watched by interested spectators. Once this was achieved the apprentice was grabbed and held down while the master farrier cut a fringe in the lower edge of his pupil's muleskin shoeing apron.

This signified that he was now considered worthy to work at the anvil without supervision and the fringe of his apron could be used to flick the hot iron scalings away. Still held firm, the apprentice submitted to having a nail hammered into the heel of his boot until he cried out 'Beer', acknowledging that he would pay for a pint for every witness of the ceremony.

For the next four years Bert's status was that of journeyman or improver, not yet qualified to call himself a master smith.

By the time that the seven years of his training were complete Britain was at war and, believing that 'Kitchener Needed Him', Bert volunteered as a farrier in the Royal Army Service Corps.

The gentle countryman who had seldom seen the sea found himself in a sinking troopship, cutting panicky mules loose and swimming with them to some Mesopotamian beach.

Having shod untameable mules and survived the carnage of the Dardanelles, Bert came home with medals on his chest and a pair of spurs cut from the heels of Johnny Turk.

He moved into the house beside the forge and, as a master farrier, proudly nailed three reversed horse-shoes on the lintel of the door. His skill was soon recognised. The old-time horsemen, who guarded the secrets of their horse medicines so jealously, favoured Bert by passing to him their various cures and remedies.

If he had a kicking mean-tempered horse to shoe Bert put a few drops of some aromatic mixture on his hand, stroked the beast from the nostril, up along the arch of its neck, down across the withers to the hoof he wanted to shoe. He would sometimes calm a horse by breathing in its nostrils and could gentle a horse as opposed to breaking it in. In all his years he never needed to hobble a horse or throw it to get it shod.

Regularly each morning at 6.30 the smithy shutters opened and, like some tocsin bell, Bert's hammer striking the anvil as he turned iron bar into horse-shoes warned the surrounding countryside that the new day had begun.

He worked in close conjunction with the wheelwright and shoeing the wheels was a spectacular procedure, involving the services of two men and a boy. Behind the 'Pant'us' — the partitioned part of the smithy where the horses were actually shod — was a circular steel plate with a centre spindle on which the wooden wheel was clamped.

The iron rim, cut a fraction smaller than the perimeter of the wheel, was put through an iron-bending machine rather like an old-fashioned mangle with three rollers, then shut and placed in a nearby circular pit piled high with faggots of kindling wood.

The fire burned fiercely until the iron rim was cherry red with heat. It was lifted from the fire with long-handled tongs. If the heat was exactly right the iron would expand to fit the wheel. Sometimes it required a touch of the hammer before it bedded in.

Immediately the rim was in position, and before the hot iron set the wood alight, it was cooled off with wet sacking and buckets of water. As the iron contracted it fitted tight upon the wheel.

Bert and old Humph the wheelwright would listen to a farm cart trundling along the village street and without seeing it know if it was one of theirs.

Prize-winning Clydesdales, racehorses, gipsy ponies, donkeys, Bert shod them all. Pompous landowners knew better than to treat the craftsman who shod their hunters as anything less than equal.

Tongued-tied farmhands smouldering under injustice confided in Bert as he replated their hoes and in his quiet way he set things right with their employers.

Repairing a leaky kettle was as much a matter of pride to Bert as was the wrought iron arch he fashioned when electricity was connected to the church. Almost secretively, the light above the churchyard gate was suspended from Bert's handiwork.

The age of farm horses passed and the shoeing side of the business dwindled to become almost non-existent.

Nevertheless, mechanically minded farmers realised that Bert could repair, renew or remake broken equipment cheaply with no waiting and no fuss.

If this happened to be fiction Bert would have lived to reap the reward of contentment and a ripe old age. He didn't. Coal dust, which demands the sacrifice of miners' lungs when first it is hewn, made Bert pay the price of working in the pollution of a smoke-filled forge.

The smithy was demolished and few things remain to show that Bert existed at all.

Above the churchyard gate there is an arch with climbing vines of flowers and fruit that look so real that each veined leaf appears to have been in some strange way bewitched and turned to iron and there are three reversed horseshoes, pyramid-fashion, above a cottage door.

Nelson

Nelson is a very old one-eyed donkey. He has long droopy ears and a coat that appears to have suffered innumerable attacks by maternity-minded moths.

His doleful, docile appearance is deceptive. That which Nelson misses with his flying heels, he catches with a sharp nip from his yellow teeth.

For years he belonged to Ikey, an itinerant who used to accompany the corn-threshing outfits from farm to farm. These 'threshing johnnies' slept rough in barns and sheds wherever the machine was working and where Ikey bedded down, his donkey slept too.

If objecting workmates demanded that Nelson should be turned out for the night, his continuous sleep-destroying braying made them change their minds. He would obey no-one but Ikey and sensible people kept well clear of both Nelson's front end and his rear.

When the threshing season finished, Ikey and the donkey would sometimes occupy a shepherd's decrepit hut, tucked away behind the dry-stone wall that divides the upland meadows from the open moorland of High Common.

Ikey looked like a character from the Old Testament.

He was a powerfully built man with a black beard, bushy eye-brows and dark penetrating eyes. Unlike most of the threshing johnnies, he was clean and tidily clothed.

He was uncommunicative, had a strange accent and whistled haunting, foreign-sounding tunes.

The fact that he was a 'furriner' explained the strangeness of his ways.

And he had strange ways. Having quietened a rampaging stallion and cured a horse which the vet had advised to be destroyed, he had the reputation of being a 'horse charmer'. There was nothing magical about this, there were old horsemen who knew how these things were done, but that is another tale.

To the village children Ikey was the local bogey man and many a recalcitrant offspring was threatened with being 'given to Ikey for his donkey's dinner'.

At threshing time it was a somewhat chastening thought to know that Ikey and the donkey were sleeping in the chaffhouse by the barn.

The cumbersome procession of the threshing outfit travelled very slowly on the narrow country roads. A chuntering traction engine with massive wheels hissed steam and smelled of coal smoke and hot oil. This pulled the high, wide, box-shaped threshing machine, invariably painted red and tarpaulin-sheeted against the wet.

Attached to the back of the thresher by a massive iron towbar was the engine driver's mobile home, a wooden caravan like an old-time seaside hut, trundling along on wooden, iron-banded wheels.

Lashed behind this came the baling machine, piled high with straw to keep its canvas feed sheets dry. The road vibrated as they passed. Bringing up the rear were the threshing johnnies wheeling ancient bicycles or trudging along in broken hobnailed boots. Last of all came Ikey, leading Nelson harnessed to a low-sprung cart.

A traction engine had an insatiable thirst. If the water trough or tap was more than a hosepipe length away it was a treadmill task to keep the monster from running dry.

The engine driver was in charge of the operation. He saw that the countless pulley wheels and drive belts were working properly, supervised the grading of the grain and kept the gauges of his highly polished engine at their correct levels, but never went on top of the threshing machine.

Only two people were allowed up there, the bond cutter and the feeder. A farmhand pitched the sheaves from the corn stack across to Ikey, who was the bond cutter. He wielded a murderous curved knife to cut the binder twine that held the sheaf together, then tossed the loosened sheaf across to the feeder, who fed it into the revolving drums of the machine.

Through a process of flailing and sieving the grain passed down through chutes into two hundredweight sacks hooked on to the front of the machine.

The straw that came out of the back and passed on through the machine did not emerge as the 'square egg' straw bale that one sees today. This was tied into long straight-stalked baled straw that would thatch a roof.

The chaff or outer casing of the corn husk and the rough straw 'cavings' were disgorged underneath the machine and a relay of workers with long wooden rakes dragged it out on to sacking carrying cloths.

This was a dusty unpleasant task for if oats were being threshed the chaff was so light that it would blow all round the yard and the long 'bearded' spikes on barley chaff irritated and stuck into one's skin.

The threshing machine made a deep melodious humming sound and with every sheaf that was consumed, it alternated key. This built up a rhythm, setting a pace by which the whole outfit worked.

NELSON

During the threshing season Nelson grew fat on fodder from the farms and surreptitious feeds of oats but in early summer Ikey and his donkey would disappear for weeks on end.

It was during one of Ikey's absences that Miss Mattie, a retired lady, acquired a broken-winded horse. She had encountered a travelling tinker ill-treating it along the lane and in her brisk, efficient way had put the fear of the law in the poor man but ended £10 poorer and the owner of a sick and lousy horse.

That evening Ikey appeared outside the gate.

"I'll look to that 'roarer' you have bought missus," he said. Miss Mattie showed him to the outhouse where the sick horse lay.

"My life!" Ikey exclaimed, then went inside and closed the outhouse door. Next morning Ikey was nowhere to be seen but the horse was up and feeding, breathing normally and free from lice.

Thereafter, bundles of fodder and straw would be tossed over the hedge of the small meadow by the house.

This went on for years, long after the threshing machines had given way to combine harvesting. No words passed between Miss Mattie and Ikey, yet one morning Miss Mattie found a grubby envelope on her front door mat.

Inside were banknotes, and the cryptic message,

"Going to my home. I told Nelson he is yours."

She found Nelson grazing with her own old horse and his harness in the low sprung cart inside the gate.

Ikey never returned and, although Nelson would allow no-one to harness him to the cart, he let Miss Mattie put his halter on.

She alone can coax him from his stubborn moods. He seems to settle down for months on end, but at times develops a nomadic urge and breaks out to wander far away.

Invariably Miss Mattie has to retrieve him from someone's stackyard. He stands immobile, refusing to be coaxed until she appears and takes him home.

Last week, when mist clung to the valley all day long, Nelson went missing again. Hugh the hill farmer heard him braying pitifully up on High Common and found him standing in the doorway of the old shepherd's hut.

When Hugh eventually got inside the hut to mend the broken door he realised that some vagrant had been using it, for the old iron stove was warm.

For once Nelson neither bit nor kicked, but allowed Hugh to stroke his neck and lead him home by the forelock of his mane. To use Hugh's words, it fair gave him the creeps.

He reckons that the poor silly old donkey thought he would find someone he knew up there, but an animal as unintelligent as a donkey would never go out searching for a long-departed friend.

Or would he? I don't know.

Stay there till I get back

One would never imagine that Will, placidly pedalling to the post office for his pension, could create a minor panic.

Yet nothing has caused so much excitement since the forestry tractor driver tipped a trailer-load of firewood over Tom Grommett's backyard fence and drove away, leaving Tom's missus trapped in the outside privy with a ton of tops and butts piled against the door.

Will rides pretty high in the saddle, his bike being a Home Guard relic issued at the time when his anti-invasion orders were that he should cycle up the hill and defend Britain and the water-tower against the advancing Nazis with a sharpened bill-hook.

Nowhere does Will ride more slowly than when he passes Plough Cottage, an ancient wattle and daub house with a thatched roof which has changed owners several times since it was sold for seventy-five pounds when the village saddler died.

The latest owner has pulled down, built up and altered the

126

old place with more enthusiasm than skill.

It took him some time before he learned that country craftsmen won't be rushed. One does not try to convert a thatcher to a time and motion routine on a frosty morning when the dressed straw is difficult to yelm. Nor does one mention dirty words like plastic straw.

When he confided to the landlord of the Hare and Hounds that he intended to extend the latest extension to make a loggia and a patio, Will was able to report that these fancy-sounding additions were nothing more than a lot of poles and an unevenly paved back yard.

Will reckons that it is all this foreign travel that gives some people such ideas.

As Will slowed down for his weekly look over Plough Cottage garden wall last Thursday, he heard a curious echoing sound that he described as being 'something like that radio chap that busts his charts'.

Will held on to the top of the wall to keep his balance and turned his good ear towards the sound. There was no one in the garden and nothing looked amiss although the paving slabs of the patio looked more uneven and had a hole in the middle. Perhaps that blamed-fool-new-chap was building a fountain or a pool.

The second time Will heard the sound he realised that it was coming from the hole.

As soon as he walked on the wobbling paving stones to investigate Will knew that the owner of Plough Cottage had discovered that it had a well.

Leaning precariously over the void, Will could see him standing on a sloping wooden sleeper a dozen feet below. Beneath him was some murky looking water.

"Well I never. What are you doing down there?" Will couldn't think of anything else to say.

"Get me out," the answer echoed up.

"You just bide quiet and I'll see what I can do." Will is getting too old for this sort of caper, but slowly and methodically he placed a ladder across the hole and found a tow rope in the boot of the owner's car.

It barely reached the upstretched hands and as Will explained, if he tried to pull unaided he would fall in too and there wasn't room for the pair of them. He hauled the rope back up and, in a moment of inspiration, grabbed a pole left over from the loggia building and an old horse collar which hung on the garage wall, a relic of the days when the building had been the saddler's shop.

With the pole on one end of the rope and the collar on the other, Will crawled back along the ladder and painstakingly placed the pole across the rungs then lowered the horse collar down the well.

"Now you just haul yourself up a bit and put your legs through the collar. You can dangle there, safe and comfy as a babby on a swing till I get back with someone as is heftier than I."

As soon as he could get enough breath to pedal his bike Will rode to raise the alarm to everyone he passed before he reached the Hare and Hounds.

Some of us dialed 999. The poor man was soon hoisted out of the well and a small crowd stood watching the several fire brigade appliances and police cars that dashed to the scene.

They discovered that there was at most a foot of water in the well. One neighbour reckons that the wailing sirens and general disturbance have made her free-range poultry egg-bound all this week.

The chap from Plough Cottage bought his rescuers a drink in the Hare and Hounds.

Even old Harry Applethorn, who tends to do his oldest inhabitant bit with strangers, was treated to a pint.

The shallowness of the water in the well was becoming something of a joke until Harry Applethorn upset everything by remarking that if yonder chap had fallen down a hole not more than twenty feet in depth, it was the rainwater tank that he had found and not the well.

"That be nigh on a hundred foot from bottom to top. So deep that when I was an unbreeched boy they used a horse to turn the capstan and drawed the water up through pipes made of elm they was, and neither water nor frost affected them. Many a time I was put on the old horse's back as it plodded round and round."

The man from Plough Cottage hadn't bargained on having one well, much less two.

With all the alterations no-one could remember the exact location of the well. There had been loads of rubble and topsoil dumped on the garden and, being a town-bred chap, he could see no way of discovering where it was.

When he was told to get Walter working with his twigs his disbelief showed on his face. Water divining? He had always thought it to be folk-lore, archaic mumbo-jumbo. Nevertheless he would be grateful for anyone who might help educate him in country ways.

At first Walter's forked hazel rod found the course of the water main, then lay unresponsive in his hands until he clambered over a pile of rubble.

The twig dipped and jerked and Walter stuck a marking peg in the ground.

Digging to find an old well is no job for one man or even two. At such times everyone lends a hand. They worked in a circle some way out from the peg and dug down until they found a ring of flagstones where the horses used to walk round and soon after struck the worm-ridden wood of the lid of the well.

Everyone's rubbish is being tipped down Plough Cottage well.

The spring interior mattress and old fridge that a passing motorist deposited in the vicarage hedge, old sinks, demolished pig-pounds. At this rate we could be in with a fighting chance in the tidiest village stakes.

There is one sobering thought. Piped water was a rare

amenity in the country until about forty or fifty years ago.

Most rural houses and groups of cottages depended on a well.

The majority of wells were haphazardly sealed, covered over with soil and promptly forgotten.

Should you have acquired the cottage of your dreams, do establish that you have nothing more lethal than fairies at the bottom of your garden, and not a slug-infested well.

Granny
Morgan's pride

'Sale This Day.' A notice-board tied to the gate-post directs buyers to the auction and Barn Field gateway is becoming a tyre-churned pool of mud.

In the last few weeks of his leasehold old Mr. Morgan cleared out the farm buildings and now the accumulated tools of a lifetime are set out in lots across Barn Field.

Dairy utensils, Granny Morgan's pride, stand rain-soaked and mud bespattered, ready to be sold. Sheltered in the empty cart-shed, her heavy farmhouse furniture, polished with love and beeswax down the years, collects grime and finger-marks from the woodworm-seeking hands.

The massive old kitchen table serves as a rostrum for the auctioneer, scrubbed whitewood desecrated by mud-clogged boots.

The auctioneer raps on the old milk churn with his gavel and the sale begins. So does the rain.

The first few sundry lots are a jumble of old pitchforks, scrap metal and feeding troughs. The auctioneer's monotonous chant, gibberish to the uninitiated, pushes the bidding along.

"Lot 12. One cheese butt with lid." A sale porter holds up a round wooden tub drilled with small holes. No one bids.

"Come, I won't waste time on unimportant items. Who will say 20p." Still no one accepts the auctioneer's offer and Granny, glaring beneath an umbrella, seems ready to prod him for giving offence.

Her cheese butt unimportant? Such ignorance could only come from a town-bred man.

Granny Morgan, perpetual motion in a floral wrap-around pinny and arch-supported shoes! Ageless, seemingly no older than the day she scorned my up-bringing because at twelve years old no-one had taught me to make cheese.

"My dear soul, you shall learn this very week," she said. I knew better than to argue.

Outside the sun was shining, but the small amount of sunlight that filtered through the thick glass of Granny Morgan's dairy was diffracted by ivy branches trailing across the panes.

It gave me the goose-pimply sensation of being inside a chilly green bottle. I watched her lift the cheese butt on to a trestle and line it with a muslin cloth.

The bowls of milk and rennet that she had set to 'curd' were tipped into the butt and I was instructed to set a pan underneath to catch the drips and to 'poke a skewer at they old holes so that the whey do run off quick'.

The lid was placed in the top of the butt and a seven pound weight put on that. Each day Granny twisted the muslin cheesecloth tighter and at the end of the week she tested it to see if it was ready by pressing her finger on the top.

"When 'tis neither mish-mushy nor too hard, you takes the cheese from the cloth and roughs it all around with a knife to give it a firm crust. You puts 'un to ripen on an open-slatted shelf or wraps it in clean muslin and hangs it from a beam out of nibbling reach of they old meece."

I begrudged the lost hours of playing time, not realising the compliment I had been paid.

Granny's cheese equalled Stilton at its best and cheese-making is an art that is often only divulged by one generation to the next.

"For the last time, 20p for the cheese butt." I brushed a raindrop from my forehead with my sale catalogue and the auctioneer's gavel rapped on the milk churn. "All done and sold at 20p." I still don't know if I intended to bid or not.

The next lot. "One barrel butter churn with stand", was an instrument of destiny where one of the local lassies was concerned.

Ethel, a village girl, used to help Granny Morgan with the dairy work. They made butter on two days of the week but when the Saturday churning was finished Ethel was free to go home.

Ethel had a boy-friend, a broad-shouldered lad with brilliantined black hair and a tendency to smelly feet. As she churned the butter Ethel dreamed of the day when she would have the right to wash his socks.

Their romance was a pretty torrid affair by local standards, insofar as she rode home from work each night on the cross-bar of his bike and they went to the pictures together every Saturday afternoon.

They saved enough money to put down the deposit on a ring and planned to visit the jewellers on their next trip into town.

The next Saturday was cold and frosty and try as Ethel might the cream would not turn to butter in the churn. She was still turning the handle as the bus went into town.

Her Romeo met another girl in the pictures and from then on, Ethel walked home from work alone.

For weeks Ethel salted the butter with her tears, her love-life thwarted by a butter churn. Now she is the wife of a prosperous American and flies home every year to see her Mum.

She sure would have raised a bid in gratitude to see the old barrel churn had she not been Stateside today.

Now the tractor and heavier implements are being sold and are bid for by the lifting of an eyebrow, the nod of a head or a gentleman pretending to take out a hanky to blow his nose.

Old Mr. Morgan confides that the potato digger has sold for almost double the price that he first paid, so he thinks it has earned its keep.

If there is a more god-forsaken job than planting potatoes, it must be picking them up but when an old neighbour has a crop that is spoiling to be harvested, everyone lends a hand.

As Granny Morgan says, 'tatty-upping' is a hungry-making job and her 'helper's dinner' almost compensated for acquiring a hairpin bend for a back. She served up cheese and potatoe pie; baked apples, cored and filled with spiced brown sugar; vanilla junket with grated nutmeg and enormous quantities of scalding hot, sweet tea. All of which is both easy on the purse and time and marvellous to eat.

It seems unbelievable that no-one will eat a 'tatty-upping' dinner at Granny Morgan's kitchen table after today. The last lot is 'all done and sold'. The buyers are departing and lorries and loaded trailers ooze their way out through the gate.

Granny and old Mr. Morgan look across the fields of the little farm that will now become part of a vast farming complex, then walk across to lock the door of the empty farmhouse.

The relentless rain beats a tattoo on the old kitchen table, mud-covered and abandoned in Barn Field.

So long
at the fair

Dan's wife said that he could please himself, she would gladly accept a lift home from the town. Her feet were near worn out with 'trapesing' around the fair, and the afternoon bus had 'been and gone and not come past'.

Dan hesitated, then got in the car, muttering that he couldn't abide women drivers and could have quite easily walked.

Overcoming apprehension, he settled in his seat.

"I grant that fair-going is a tiring old job," he admitted, "but the Horse Fair is nothing like it was.

"There were few high days and holidays in the poverty-stricken times folk call 'the good old days', nor was there much cause for jollification. Horse Fair week was something different though.

"We dubbined our boots, strip washed down and changed our shirts though t'were only midweek, then, spruced up like bantam cocks, we went off into town.

"Them as was fit walked, the young 'uns were pushed and

MARTIN LAW.

the farmers lent their wagons and teams to take such old folk as wanted to go to the fair.

"The town fairly 'eaved with folks. Gipsy wagons were pulled on to the cobbles one side of the market cross and the fairground caravans on t'other. There were some rare old fights between the two.

"Horses by the dozen waited to be auctioned off in Market Street and the pens in the cattle market were full of stock.

"There were swingboats, stalls and sideshows, freaks and fortune tellers and a chap as would pull your teeth for six-pence. Of course it was a hiring and firing fair in those days, as well I know."

Dan fell silent, drawing hard on a foul smelling short-stemmed pipe and reflecting on the Horse Fair as it was just before he was fourteen.

That year Dan went blithely to the fair wearing new boots and his father's cut down coat. He took scant notice of the conversation his father was holding with a gentleman farmer.

His mother told him to mind his manners and say his prayers and then Dan realised that he was a fully fledged stable-hand, engaged for the sum of £10 a year with free bed and board plus one pair of boots, a pair of breeches and a new shirt every year.

His straw bed was in the stable loft which he shared with the wagoner and a groom. Meals were eaten in the back kitchen of the farmhouse.

Sunday meant mutton for dinner. For the rest of the week 'pot-wallopers' were the staple diet. These were a mixture of flour, rough suet and water made into a solid dough, wrapped in a cloth and boiled for hours.

There was much competition and rivalry as to which farm had the smartest turn-out at the fair and by the time the next Horse Fair came round Dan was very much 'one of the lads'.

He rode beside the wagoner in a newly painted farm cart, their team of shire horses high-stepping their polished hooves and jingling the burnished brasses of their harness.

Dan had helped to braid their manes and tails with red, white and blue ribbon, 'wearing the worsted' as the old horsemen said.

He had to hand most of his first year's wages to his mother, but with a whole florin in his pocket Dan felt as affluent as a lord as he strolled round the side shows.

He thought he might risk one penny on the moving picture machines and chose one labelled 'Frolics by the Sea'.

Dan had never seen the sea and, while he was mildly interested in some ladies with naked forearms spasmodically splashing in the water up to the bottom of their knee-length bloomers, he was so fascinated by the jerking waves of the sea that he invested in another pennyworth.

He never got full value for his money, for a resounding thump on his back almost sent his eyeballs through the eyepiece, then he was hauled upright to face his 'maister's' wife, a righteous lady who railed at him for being licentious and lustful.

She ordered him to go and mind her pony which was tied up to a hitching ring on the back wall of the chapel, well away from the temptations of the fair.

A very gloomy Dan leaning against the chapel wall watched the 'maister's' wife and the wagoner approaching, the wagoner carrying a set of harness.

"Fancy," said the 'Missus', "I've just bought a second set of harness for the pony and it's almost identical to the one he's wearing now."

"What harness?" asked Dan. The pony had been standing with just a halter on when he had arrived. He got one hiding for the harness being stolen and another because the 'Missus' had bought it back.

Three hidings on one Horse Fair day Dan could stand, but to be made to put the remainder of his florin in the chapel poor-box was too much. Daniel joined the ranks of the unemployed.

There were two kinds of horse-trading at the fair. While

138

the auctioneers were selling horses which were being paraded up and down Market Street, in Three Bells Lane the gipsies and dealers conducted a horse sale of their own.

Horses sold cheaper there, but it took a knowledgeable man to find a real bargain. All the greasy-legged, lousy, workshy nags were there with the horse-fakers.

Old horses with grey muzzles walnut-leaf-stained brown, and with filed down teeth stood looking fit for nothing but the knacker's yard until a likely customer approached.

As the dealer engaged the client in conversation the horse would suddenly become very lively and muster a fast trot down the lane.

"Good for years of work," was one phrase.

"Horse-jollying" was another. It was simply and sadistic-ally achieved.

For days before, the wretched horse would have its head close tied between two stakes and be driven frantic by the dealer's assistant hammering on a bucket with a stick or rattl-ing a tin full of stones inside a sack, just under its nose.

At the sale the demented creature had only to see the same man standing with the terrifying bucket or sack in his hand to become lively and agitated. Nothing would look more innocent to the mug out to buy a cheap horse.

Any 'gorgio' buying a horse was fair game, but horse-trading between gipsies was different. Almost ritualistic hagg-ling with raised voices, posturing, much shaking of heads and walking away.

Just as suddenly a price would be agreed and the bargain sealed with a slapping of the transactors' hands.

The seller always returned a silver coin for 'luck money'.

This the buyer spat on, rubbed and placed in his pocket to ensure good fortune on the deal.

Dan recalled that the farm-hands often bought clothes from the stalls at the fair. His wife said that she had bought a bargain that very day.

There was rustling of paper in the back seat of the car

and the conversation went something like this:

"Whatever is them then, mother. Let us have a look."

There was a disgusted grunt.

"They are tights Daniel, three pairs for twelve pence."

"Tights!" Dan exploded. "You have as many brains as a pig has got pockets. Silly old gal. Two pair has one leg shorter than t'other and the third was made to fit the shape of a little old toad.

"Ain't you been going to the fair long enough not to buy old 'rubbidge'?"

"At least I haven't bought any Wonder pills." Dan's wife deflated him with a glance and went on to recall the year that some chap calling himself Doctor Watson sold special tablets, the formula of which contained some mysterious ingredients derived from the glands of apes.

They were guaranteed to put new life in men.

It attracted a lot of custom to the 'doctor's' stall at the fair.

The following morning several village men stood self-consciously waiting to attend the weekly surgery held in the back room at the post office. Each one carried a container, ranging from jam-jars to flower vases, all containing bright green liquid.

"Yes," said Dan's wife, "and there wasn't a wife among us that didn't go in fear and dread of having a green baby all that year."

"Women!" snorted Dan. "They do say that at one time a man could auction off his wife! No, the fair ain't what it was!"

The fragile fortress

We fed the calves by lantern light that morning and by daybreak I had the cart loaded, Jim harnessed and stood waiting, impatient to be off.

Mum hurried across the cobbled yard, tucking stray wisps of hair up under her best velour hat, stabbing the purple cabbage-rose trimming with a lethal looking hat-pin as she went.

"Check that nothing is forgotten," she called. I checked.

Several complaining cockerels chuntered in their crates. There were eggs, butter, bushels of Blenheim apples, seven snared rabbits and mistletoe that I had cut from the apple tree in the yard. I had even remembered a horse rug and the enormous umbrella in case it rained.

Mum was the wrong shape to clamber into a two-wheeled tip-cart and no sooner was she heaved in than she wanted to get out. "Wait," she said, "I have left the shopping bags on the table." I went back and collected them, all six.

Then we were off, with Jim's hooves ringing on the roadway, gravel crunching beneath the iron-shod wheels and Mum, myself, and the horse each making individual miniature fog-banks as we breathed in the morning air.

Mum was anxious to reach the Christmas produce market early and get low lot numbers so that our items for sale would be auctioned first.

Then we could get her Christmas shopping done in time for us to get back home by dark.

Our produce went under the hammer and Mum totted up how much shopping money she had made. My seven snared rabbits and the bunches of mistletoe had earned me twelve shillings and I did mental mathematical gymnastics to divide that to buy presents for my brothers, sisters, nephews and nieces who seemed to increase in numbers every year.

Dad was no fool to opt out of driving Mum to the Christ-mas market and I knew enough to let her tackle her Christmas shopping by herself. She started off with a variety of straw and string bags hung on one arm, pursuing bargains as if she was preparing for a siege.

Hawk-eyed, she watched the grocer's scales go down and if it didn't the cowering counterhand would be denounced as 'nothing but a nip-cheese' to other customers in the market-day busy shop.

As each shopping bag got too heavy to carry she would blithely deposit it on the counter of the nearest shop, inform-ing the unsuspecting shopkeeper that she would soon be back.

Then I would retrace the route of her shopping spree, collecting the bulging bags. Sometimes she would forget which shop had been honoured with her left luggage. That morning I drove round looking for 'a place where they sold socks'.

Through the doorway of a frightfully select Gents Out-fitters and Tailoring establishment I saw Mum's overfull straw shopper on the glass-topped counter.

Right on top was a butcher's sixpenny bargain sheep's head, grinning out of a bloodstained newspaper wrapping as if it was as pleased to see Mum as she was to find it. As she explained to a youthful assistant in a celluloid collar, one 'hurdle bumper' equals two basins of brawn and three of broth, and if you have never heard of mutton brawn you didn't know my waste-not-want-not Mum.

While Mum had been shopping I had spent most of my twelve shillings and solved my Christmas present problem bidding for, and buying, a miscellaneous lot in the market.

Lumped together in a dull metal log-box with a broken lid were several china vases, a shaving mug and a pile of books.

Mum loved reading, the shaving mug would do for Dad and there appeared to be enough vases to give my sisters a present each.

'One copper log-box with sundry items' had cost eight shillings of my twelve and, in a whirl of teenage self-indulgence, I lashed out on a one and elevenpenny pair of artificial silk stockings and a pint sixed bottle of Ashes of Carnation scent at one and six.

Two hot pies and a mug of tea for Mum and me cost sixpence.

Still solvent to the extent of one penny, I hauled Mum back up into the cart and drove home along the lanes.

With Mum safely indoors I could move the log-box from under the chicken crates where I had hidden it and in the corn store examine what I had bought. The books, mostly romantic novels, would delight Mum, who loved a long weepy read.

The shaving mug when washed and polished would please Dad.

At the bottom of the lucky-dip log-box was a cardboard container and inside this were gramophone records ranging from Mozart to *The Merry Widow* and Marie Lloyd. These I felt would give Mum a Christmas bonus and I took them indoors.

There were several oven-ready chickens which had been ordered and, having spent the day shopping, we plucked and trussed them by lamplight in the kitchen after tea.

As we worked and sat there talking the conversation turned to the subject of Mum's youth.

At the age of thirteen as a scullery maid, she had shivered night after night in an unheated, unceilinged attic. From that window she could look down into the ballroom of a grand hotel.

Listening to the music and watching the dancing had brightened her unendurably drab existence and the strains of that music had echoed down her years.

"Such glittering ball-gowns, such beautiful waltzes as you would never believe," she said.

As she sat in her old cover-all hessian apron plucking chickens, with the feathers falling into an old tin bath, I put one of the 'bonus records' on and the lamp-lit kitchen was filled with the music of Lehar's *Merry Widow* waltz.

It was soon filled with feathers too, for Mum dropped|the chicken and whirled me round and round the kitchen table, teaching me how to dance.

On the next day Christmas preparations began in earnest.

The kitchen range gobbled fuel like a starving monster and no sooner was the oven emptied of a batch of baking than it was filled with clean dry bricks. Heated, these would be put in old stockings and used to air and warm the extra beds.

There were bedroom fires to lay and logs to carry, but none of the extra work mattered. Mum's children who had grown and gone away were coming home for Christmas and the family would once again be safe within the fortress of her love.

Each year I rustled up enough of the festive spirit to wel come Uncle Fred but my quota of goodwill stopped some-what short of Cousin Daisy his daughter and Aunt Bertha, his domineering wife. They were by our standards wealthy and often condescended to spend a 'good old country Christmas' at my hard-pressed parents' expense.

There were always pre-visit 'don't put mice in your aunt's

slippers' lectures and I was forbidden to tell Daisy tales of headless horsemen and vampire bats. But on principle I had collected four dead spiders and deposited them in Daisy's single bed.

The house was alive with fire-lit welcome then, in a Christmas Eve mistletoe-kissing uproar, the family circle was complete. In our under-the-eaves little bedroom, Daisy displayed her crepe-de-chine French knickers and asked if I had noticed how like Ginger Rogers she had grown. To me she was just a chubby-built girl with acne and steel curlers in her hair.

She said that she had brought me a present. I conceded that she had a surprise waiting, knowing that she had yet to find the spiders in her bed.

"Yours is a pair of real silk stockings," she told me and pride demanded that I found something to give her in return.

All that I had to sacrifice was my pint sized bottle of Ashes of Carnation scent and I begrudged every farthing of the one and six that it had cost.

The blacksmith's son had volunteered to mend the copper log-box for me and on Christmas morning he brought it back, polished and burnished for me, an additional present for my Mum.

Daisy, reeking of Ashes of Carnation, stood simpering under the mistletoe, waiting to be kissed.

"Phew, have they been making you carry mildewed hay?" the blacksmith's son enquired then kissed me, needing no mistletoe at all.

Christmas passed in a plum pudding haze of laughter until it was, by family tradition, time for Mum to sing *The End Of A Perfect Day*. Then, candle-lit, we went to bed.

The fires in the bedroom grates would turn to cold ash by morning and like that ash Mum's world would soon be scattered to the winds. The fragile fortress, defended by her unselfish love, had withstood the onslaughts of another year and her family circle was complete.

Paradise

Paradise is a large white jug patterned with roses and forget-me-nots.

It is full of strong, sweet tea and is carried by my mother.

A yellow straw shopping bag nearly as deep as I am high drags on the dusty path as I struggle along the lane, fascinated by the sun hat perched precariously on my mother's head, defying the huge hatpins and bobbing up and down as she hurries on in front of me.

We walk between the poplar trees, their leaves rustling in the breeze like the sea on a shingle beach.

By the half-built haystack she spreads out the faded blue cloth. The wagon wheels beat out a rhythm as the haymakers come, eager for their meal.

Cottage loaves broken into quarters, hunks of cheese and onions that set my mouth on fire and me too happy to refuse because I am near my Dad, sharing his tea.

The warmth of the sun, the laughter of the men who tell my mother that she makes her cottage loaves to match her shape.

The hayfield scent, mingling sweet briar and honeysuckle. That is a sort of paradise.

Paradise is a March night, with the sky so filled with stars that a little star shoots across the sky to find a less crowded space to shine. In Twelve Acre meadow among the thatched hurdles the flock of sleeping ewes stir and rise as they see the lantern at the gate.

They walk towards me and we pass the time of night.

Here and there the proud mums nudge their lambs and tell them to lay still.

Outside the circle of the light, a plaintive call. One old ewe has rolled over on her back and cannot rise.

There, beside the quiet hedgerow where primroses shine white against the moss, we wait. She has no fear of me and I do not fear the night.

When at last she stands, her lamb beside her, the gate is quietly closed and thick cocoa, drunk beside a kitchen fire, drives out the March chill so that I go to bed with easy mind.

Paradise is a copper beech tree standing like a bride with auburn hair. The blossom-covered cherry orchard is her wedding dress and the hawthorn banks her train.

Paradise is a field of April wheat having its hair combed.

Bess, the half-blind mare, pulls the light harrow but suddenly stops.

No amount of 'Come on' or 'Giddup' will make her budge.

In front of her great shire hooves is a skylark's nest and no amount of straightening up will hide the fact that in the middle of the field's lined tapestry there is a corrugated curve.

Paradise is sheep-dipping time when the newly shorn sheep, looking like city gents caught office-bound in underpants and vest, are dipped in custard-coloured wash to drive away the monster-looking tick.

The local constable, cattle records all duly checked and signed, will lean against the five-barred gate, roasting in his serge, determined to uphold the dignity of the law.

He fights the desire to sleep brought on, no doubt, by the tumbler of home-made wine he declared to be as harmless as the milk it stood by on the dairy slab.

He watches as we each in turn get wet with splashing spray and all the flock are dipped but one.

Bill the ram, whose head can split a stake and who once chased a would-be suitor, all Sunday dressed, to monkey climb a tree and kept him there all afternoon.

Whatever else the constable will enter in his books, he can be sure that no tick or warble fly will molest him on his journey home, for Bill decides that they will both take the waters and charges smartly from behind, sending the policeman jet propelled into the dip.

Soon after, hysterical with mirth, I pump clean water from the well over the head of the law, now minus tunic and dignity and wondering what to tell his sergeant.

Paradise is an old white house with barn-like door flung open wide all day, although everyone is busy round the farm.

No harm would come from folks who might come by. The gipsy family who turn up like magic every year in early June and stay until the harvest's in the barn would never steal from such as we.

This is a place of laughter, hard work and content, although poverty is only a ruined summer's crop away.

Paradise is another time, another place, before little men with measuring tapes and marking posts tore out the heart of Twelve Acre field and built the rows of three-up, three-down with bath and outside w.c.

Where the song thrush sang in the hawthorn bush, the ice-cream van ding-dongs its tin tune chimes.

The copper beech is gone and yet the council man plants saplings to be hacked to bits by children who don't care.

The barn that generations of my kind stacked high with corn now houses roadmen's brooms and the old house, defiled with plastic tiles and stainless steel, its dark beams hidden like a shameful past, will still stand strong when all the rest are slums.

The occupants can never really know what spring and summer really mean, except that cricket alternates with football on T.V.

The tenant planting up his hanky of a patch will never know that the root he curses as he breaks his fork was a tree that once bore fruit fit to send to London for a King.

And a minute's walk away the old farm lane, all overgrown with bramble, leads to nowhere any more.

It used to lead to the chestnut spinney, notorious since the time when Jack the shepherd was full of beer and song one Saturday night. He decided that a nap would help his head and went to sleep upon a pile of chestnut poles.

Made restless by the beer and deeply asleep at that, he was found firmly wedged by Miss Woods, the spinster organist Matins-bound.

Her efforts to release him and the fact that eucharist was said instead of sung that day made a tale that still makes people smile.

The lane stops dead where, on concrete stilts, the motorway, Common Market bound, strides across the country to the coast and paradise is gone from here.

Paradise is like the old white jug smashed a thousand ways and unless there is another time and another place, can never be regained.